JONATHAN DAVIES
CODE BREAKER

JONATHAN DAVIES

CODE BREAKER

WITH PETER CORRIGAN

BLOOMSBURY

First published in 1996 by
Bloomsbury Publishing Plc
2 Soho Square
London W1V 6HB

Copyright © by Jonathan Davies 1996

A copy of the CIP entry for this book is available from the British Library

ISBN 0 7475 2551 X

10 9 8 7 6 5 4 3 2 1

Typeset by Hewer Text Composition Services, Edinburgh
Printed in Britain by Clays Ltd, St Ives plc

To Karen

Acknowledgements

I am very grateful to my family and friends and the coaches, players and members of the media whose words and memories about my life and my rugby career have been so freely used in the telling of this story. The help we've had is typical of the kindness and support I've received from so many in both codes. In a team game no individual player can achieve anything without the ability, the sweat and the courage of all those around him and when I was awarded the MBE in 1995, I felt I shared the honour with a large number of rugby people. Putting together this book has made me aware of how many that involves and how big a debt I owe to others.

My thanks are also due to the photographers who've provided me with a permanent record of my career and who've given me permission to reproduce their copyright photographs: Mike Brett, Frank Coppi, N. Fairhurst, Mike Flynn, Andrew Varley, Gerald Webster.

Contents

CHAPTER 1

One Rugby World

I consider myself to be a citizen of the rugby world – one world, not two as has been the case for a hundred years or more.

I am not overlooking the fact that rugby league and rugby union are two distinct games, and neither am I suggesting they shouldn't remain so. But when I look back on a career that has stretched across both codes, and across the world as well, I don't see any barrier, any great divide.

All I see are snatches of memorable action involving rugby players of varying skills and shapes and sizes, great stadiums and roaring crowds. I sometimes have to pause to work out which piece of play came from which code.

The two greatest teams I have seen in my life were the Australian rugby league team who toured Britain in 1982 and the New Zealand team of 1988, who were a superior version of the team who won the rugby union World Cup in 1987 and, in my opinion, even better than the All Blacks who won the Tri-Nations tournament in July 1996. The fact that they played different games mattered much less than the brilliant standard of rugby they achieved. In my opinion, they revealed the skill, strength and pace to move a rugby ball like it's never been moved before or since. Under whose rules they did it doesn't seem to matter.

The fact that those giants would be debarred from meeting was an insult to the name of sport; one of many disgraces that were allowed to fester in the game of rugby.

The implications of the International Rugby Board's historic decision to make union open and to make honest and acceptable players of us all brought many months of controversy and confusion to the administration of the game across the world and within the individual unions.

1

The bitter arguments took the emphasis off the human aspect. We saw a rush of union players grabbing massive contracts as if they were afraid the authorities would change their minds. Who can blame them? The most important part of rugby is the playing of it, and when everything settles down, it will be recognized that the most important new word in rugby is not money; it is freedom.

I was the first to be allowed to take advantage of it. The 154th Welsh international to turn to rugby league over the past century, I was the first to be allowed to re-cross the bridge. Returning has proved to be no easier than leaving, but that is not a complaint. I have only to think of the many who have suffered exile and persecution because they decided to take honest reward for their rugby skills to realize how fortunate I am.

I consider it a privilege to represent them, to be the first to experience what they could only dream about. For me, unfortunately, it has been more like a nightmare. My wife Karen and I came back to rebuild our life in Wales, to ensure our children grew up there and spoke Welsh. I also wanted to be on home ground to fight my battle to re-establish myself as a rugby union player. Like all sportsmen eager to be amongst the big names and the great moments, I regarded that as the highest of my priorities.

But Karen was suddenly confronted by a real battle, one that brought a new and stunning perspective to our lives. Professional sportsmen, and many amateurs, too, tend to be self-centred people. But this was a situation in which my problems, my struggles to get re-accepted in a game I had forsaken, were dwarfed. When you spend hours sitting by the bedside of someone you love while they receive chemotherapy treatment, you don't think of what you are going to do next time a pass thuds into your hands – assuming, that is, you ever get a pass.

How much I was affected by it all is difficult to say. Every time I went on to the pitch Karen wanted me to do well, and I wanted to do well for her. I met a curious and mixed reaction to my return. I even fell out with a couple of old friends. There was a lot of jealousy and discontent about the jobs I was given by the Welsh Rugby Union and others. From the rugby point of view, I don't think I got a fair crack of the whip in my first six months at Cardiff, and the strangest things happened on the pitch. I thought

I'd missed an official health warning: that you can catch Aids from passing a rugby ball to someone you don't know very well.

Other people got more agitated than I did. They would come up and commiserate and rant about it being deliberate. I would just shrug it off. I never agreed it was deliberate and still find it difficult to believe it was; at least I sincerely hope it wasn't. Truth was that Karen's illness made what happened on a rugby pitch unimportant. We were fighting parallel battles, and she was doing a damn sight better in hers than I was in mine – which was really all that mattered.

But people didn't realize how difficult it was for me to adjust to union again. It was a different game from the one I'd left. It wasn't as quick and had developed a tedious nature that I could hardly cope with. Even in my short time back, thankfully, it has perked up considerably.

One thing the matches between Wigan and Bath at the end of the 1995–96 season proved was how different the two games are. In their first encounter, under league rules, Bath were wrecked. When Wigan went on to win the Middlesex Sevens, there was serious conjecture that the rugby league champions could win the union return at Twickenham. They were swept off their feet and bewildered just as Bath had been. I could have warned them. Even when you think you know union as well as I did, it takes a lot of adjustment in order for a rugby league brain to cope.

This book is not a judgement of one game against the other. Apart from taking several volumes, it would be a pointless exercise. My advice to young players is to take advantage of the freedom you've been given and try both codes.

Now that the seasons don't conflict, there are plenty of opportunities to experience a new dimension to rugby. I don't recommend a future of back-to-back seasons, but if you are going to be a professional, make sure you are in the game that suits you best and that you can enjoy most.

If they ever are to come together as one game it will be player-led. We will create a new breed of player and eventually I believe the games will blend naturally. It will make less and less sense for players of the talents of Jonah Lomu and Va'aiga Tuigamala to be kept apart.

I haven't yet made the mark in union that I wanted to. Whether I do or not, I don't feel I've played my last rugby league game. I am under contract to play in Australia in the summer of 1997, and if I'm still in one piece I intend to honour it.

When the rugby season ended in May 1996, I had spent over 21 months in continuous rugby action (I count the operating theatre as part of the rugby field). After the regular season I started with Warrington in August 1994 – in which I played 29 games and scored 292 points – I played in Australia with the North Queensland Cowboys in the summer of 1995 and took a small leap for mankind to join Cardiff in November 1995. Along the way I helped Great Britain beat Australia at Wembley with a try I consider the most important of my life; I was awarded the MBE; and I led the Welsh rugby league side to the semi-finals of the World Cup. I also became 33.

I hope it is not all over, but even now it is a rugby story that could never have been lived before and will never be lived again.

CHAPTER 2

Rubicon Re-crossed

The ending of the bitter division between rugby union and rugby league did not arrive like a flash of lightning. In the context of the hundred years war between the codes, it happened comparatively quickly, but to those who were impatient for the barriers to be torn down the great change dribbled slowly into being over a period of many months and, given the stubborn nature of the administrators involved, had a fragile feel to it even then.

The final acceptance by union that the game would have to turn professional to avoid a global disintegration was a momentous sporting decision on its own. But it carried with it the requirement for peace to be made with the arch-enemy. Union's disdainful treatment of league players, even those who'd merely had a trial for a league club, had long been morally indefensible; now it was legally so.

The announcement of a free gangway between the codes had to wait for its real impact until someone actually made use of it. To his astonishment, Jonathan Davies found himself being hustled across the unbridgeable gap to become the first rugby player to be bought back from league by a union club.

Before that could happen, another breakthrough had to be achieved. Gareth Davies, chief executive of Cardiff RFC, had to do business with Warrington RLFC. The first official contacts between the old enemies turned out to be as tense and as difficult as they were historic.

The initial meeting between Gareth Davies and Graham Armstrong, his opposite number at Warrington, took place on Wednesday 4 October 1995, in the cafeteria at Sandbach Services on the M6. The meeting should have taken place two days earlier, but Gareth had celebrated his fortieth birthday the previous weekend and his wife had treated him to a surprise trip to Ireland. Stormy weather caused the ferries to be cancelled and they were stranded in Rosslare. To Gareth's embarrassment, the meeting had to be postponed.

Gareth remembers the delicate opening of face-to-face negotiations as an arm's-length confrontation; understandable, perhaps, considering they were both dealing where no man had dealt before. He explained that Cardiff was strictly a members' club with slim resources and a cash-flow problem even before they'd negotiated what they would be paying their players under the new professional rules. Jonathan would receive no more than any other player, and certainly it would be no more than a fraction of the amount Warrington were paying him. He would get most of his income from jobs outside the club.

Even as he talked about Cardiff's difficulty in raising much of a transfer fee, Davies felt he was not eliciting much sympathy. His suspicion was confirmed when Armstrong countered that none of this had been Warrington's idea. Losing Jonathan was the last thing they wanted, because he was a vital player who would need replacing by someone equally outstanding, and they estimated his transfer value at £250,000.

Gareth Davies swallowed hard. It had taken Cardiff a lot of time and trouble to get this far, and suddenly there seemed a much longer road to travel if, indeed, it was worth going any further.

It was one of the fateful aspects of Cardiff's attempt to sign Jonathan that it should be conducted by Gareth. Seven years his senior, Gareth had long been a significant figure in Jonathan's life. Gareth had preceded his namesake out of Wales's famed outside-half factory – the Gwendraeth Valley near Carmarthen. Jonathan had followed Gareth into Gwendraeth Grammar School and watched his career blossom at Cardiff and for Wales, whom he captained and for whom he was capped 21 times. Jonathan eventually replaced him in the Welsh team in remarkable circumstances.

When he finished playing, Gareth sought a career in finance while at the same time building up an impressive reputation as a sportswriter for the Sunday Express. *No doubt this display of flair in the media world was one of the reasons he was chosen to be Head of Sport for BBC Wales. It was an enviable position for a sports lover and not the sort of job a man could be easily persuaded to forsake, but after several distinguished years he was offered a new challenge he couldn't resist.*

Cardiff RFC, one of the world's most famous rugby clubs, had attracted the patronage of Peter Thomas, a former hooker with the club whose success in business had not dimmed his passionate interest in rugby. Cardiff, in common with the Welsh game as a whole, were in the doldrums in the early 1990s, and Thomas offered a gift of £500,000 to replenish their resources. Thomas sought nothing in return apart from the appointment of a chief executive who could prepare the club for a more successful future.

Gareth Davies, who for years had been the Cardiff team's motivational heart at outside half, was invited to take on this exacting and, in those days, pioneering post. When he took over the reins at Cardiff in 1994 the prospect of running a major club was daunting enough, but what was already a tough assignment would, within a year or so, take on a fearful new dimension.

He was on holiday in Portugal in August 1995 when the International Rugby Board finally decided to recommend that the game should turn professional. He heard about it while browsing through a supermarket and the screech of his mobile phone suddenly drew the attention of the entire shop. He ducked behind a stack of tins to take the call. It was from a reporter back in Wales who asked for his reaction to the news.

The free passage between union and league had yet to be introduced but was already being spoken of as a distinct possibility when, coincidentally, Gareth and Peter Thomas met Jonathan later that month at a dinner at the new Celtic Manor golf complex to honour Ian Woosnam. The prospects of his being able to return to union were discussed in very much a hypothetical manner. Jonathan drove back to Warrington encouraged by their interest but pessimistic about the chances of such a move being possible before his playing days were over.

In September, a meeting of Cardiff's Strategic Committee – which comprised Gareth, Peter Thomas, Keith James, a lawyer, Keith Brooks, an accountant, and C.D. Williams, the chairman of Cardiff Athletic Club – decided that if the club had to face professionalism they should start thinking about strengthening the squad with one or two star players. Among the names discussed were England centre Jeremy Guscott and Jonathan.

Neither was an easy target, but although access to Jonathan would almost require an act of God at that moment, the club asked Gareth to concentrate on bringing the Welshman home.

By the time the International Board decided to allow individual unions to make their own arrangements for allowing free movement for league players, Cardiff were well ahead with cobbling together the wherewithal for what were in effect two distinct deals. The first was to raise whatever transfer fee Warrington would accept and the second was to arrange a package of jobs to ensure that Jonathan did not have to suffer a severe drop in income.

Coincidentally, Jonathan was in Cardiff when Gareth was working on the deals. The player arrived with the Welsh squad to prepare for their qualifying group matches in the Rugby League World Cup. Their hotel was within 200 yards of Cardiff's offices, and although Jonathan popped in for the odd cup of coffee and a chat, he was determined not to be distracted from his job as Welsh captain.

He had started the ball rolling by telling Warrington chairman Peter Higham of his hopes to return to Wales and of Cardiff's interest. Higham wrote to him formally stating that if he wanted to play for Cardiff, Warrington would want full compensation.

When their idea of full compensation was divulged to Gareth Davies at Sandbach Services, the Cardiff official explained that if his club pushed everything they had into the kitty he doubted if they could manage more than £30,000.

A day or two later this figure appeared in the press as if it had been a firm offer. This annoyed Gareth. He hadn't been empowered to offer anything. He was merely naming the sort of figure to which they might aspire. Either way, Warrington publicly dismissed it as derisory and there then followed exchanges between the clubs that can only be described as acrimonious. The phone was slammed down on at least one occasion.

By the time Jonathan had taken Wales to the semi-final of the World Cup against England at Old Trafford, the deal was deadlocked, with no apparent way out. When the final whistle sounded over Wales's defeat, Jonathan sank to his knees in an outward display of emotion not previously seen in his career.

When he caught up with the state of the negotiations he was, metaphorically speaking, back on his knees. 'Forget it,' he told Gareth. 'I'll bloody retire and then they'll get nothing.'

Gareth did not take it as an empty threat. He knew that Jonathan was disappointed at Warrington's attitude and that his enthusiasm at the prospect of going home had been increased by the reception he and his team had received in Wales.

Jonathan was also excited by the employment opportunities that were opening up for him. BBC Wales had lined up an extended contract for television and radio work, the WRU wanted to appoint him as development officer with the 1999 World Cup in mind, and Jewson, Cardiff's sponsors, wanted to involve him in their marketing team nationwide.

Within the Cardiff club, the idea was put forward that Jonathan ought to be encouraged to move back to Wales, join Cardiff as an amateur and leave Warrington to take legal action if they cared, or dared, to.

'It was an expression of our frustration,' recalls Gareth. 'Rugby league clubs had been raping and pillaging Welsh rugby for a century. They took some of our best players without a penny compensation to the clubs, and now that the boot was on the other foot they were trying to hold us to ransom.'

Whether Cardiff were prepared to risk court action was never tested, because two developments led to the impasse being broken. The first was a ruling by the Welsh Rugby Union who had been sympathetic from the outset to Cardiff's attempt to bring Jonathan back. It was a regulation of the Heineken League that all players had to be registered by 31 October in order to play in that season. As that deadline approached, so Warrington's bargaining power was strengthened, but Vernon Pugh, chairman not only of the WRU but of the International Board, made provision for an extension in exceptional circumstances.

That relieved some of the pressure on Gareth Davies as he fought to gather the finance he needed to complete the deal. Jewson, the nationwide builder's merchants, had been a great ally. They'd offered a contribution to the transfer fee plus a part-time job for Jonathan. But although Cardiff came up with an amount above the original £30,000 that Gareth had talked about, Warrington still turned it down as 'unacceptable'.

Then Gareth received a call from the car phone of Dr Chris Evans, whom he knew vaguely to be very wealthy and a Welsh rugby fanatic. At the age of 36, Dr Evans had become a multimillionaire through the success of a string of bioscience companies. Nevertheless, Gareth was more than a little guarded when his caller asked what the shortfall was in Cardiff's offer. He agreed to discuss the matter further at Dr Evans's home.

They spent three hours discussing Jonathan and the importance to Wales of his return. Dr Evans had been approached by several clubs hoping to receive his support, but although he was anxious to help Welsh rugby he didn't want to throw his money away on something that wasn't properly structured. He was convinced that Cardiff's bid to bring back Jonathan was worthy of his support. He rang a millionaire friend of his who lives in Switzerland, Rhondda-born John Morris, and within a few hours they were able to place at Gareth's disposal an amount they felt Warrington would not refuse.

On the evening of Sunday 29 October, Gareth telephoned the Warrington chairman with the improved offer and agreed the deal in principle. Cardiff are not willing to reveal the amounts involved or the exact nature of what was a complicated deal, even Jonathan is not fully aware of them, and the many details had to be thrashed out the following day with Armstrong and, indeed, took a few more days to finalize. But just before 10 p.m. on Monday evening, Gareth rang Jonathan's home in Widnes to tell him it was as good as settled.

Despite his fatigued relief that the end was in sight, Gareth remembers an enormous feeling of sympathy for his friend at the other end of the line.

'Bloody hell,' he thought as he replaced the receiver, 'how is he going to cope?'

It was late in the evening on Monday 30 October 1995, and on television Robbie Coltrane was ten minutes away from solving the latest murder mystery in *Cracker*. Suddenly, the ring of the telephone broke into our concentration.

'If that's a reporter, tell them I'm still at training,' I said to Karen without taking my eyes off the set.

'Tell them yourself,' she said, rudely.

Keeping my eyes on *Cracker*, I backed away towards the hall and reached for the phone, intent on a brief conversation.

Gareth Davies didn't bother to introduce himself. 'Jonathan,' he said, 'it's on.'

Karen and I never did find out what happened at the end of *Cracker*. The prospect of returning home hit us like a hurricane. It was not an unhappy hurricane. There were relatives and friends to phone with the news, plans for moving to be discussed, house-hunting and all the other domestic arrangements involved in shipping a family back home.

It was later, lying in bed and letting my mind stray into the future, that I began to get apprehensive. We were, after all, about to take another leap into the unknown. Wales was hardly new territory but I wasn't exactly sure then how I was going to earn a living or how much longer I could carry on playing. It was precisely because I wanted to carve out a career beyond the rugby pitch that the Cardiff deal appealed to me, but I was giving up a great deal of existing security. Despite my other complaints, I was on very good money at Warrington and there was the prospect of a lucrative move to Australia in 1997. Had there been an offer from rugby league involving me as a development officer, I might well have stayed.

Contrary to many reports, we were not desperately homesick. We always thought we'd end up back home but we thoroughly enjoyed ourselves during our seven years in Cheshire. Keeping contact with the family, and them with us, involved many tediously long road or train journeys, but we were happily settled and there were tears all round when we finally took our leave of our neighbours.

Neither was I still a union player at heart, one who had merely loaned himself out to rugby league. I regarded myself a league player through and through. I fancy not everyone up north accepted me as one of them, but I certainly felt completely part of the game and was proud to be connected with it.

The harsh fact was that I had to think of my future. I'd had various jobs but they all involved me having a high profile as a player. Coaching was an obvious avenue for me to explore eventually, but I wanted to acquire some other skills. Media work had always fascinated me and I knew there was an opportunity with BBC Wales to get a solid grounding in radio and television.

Since the Welsh Rugby Union were also interested in employing me to help their marketing of the 1999 World Cup, Cardiff seemed to be the right place at the right time. The fact that they were the best club in Wales at the time, and run by men I liked and respected, made it an attractive move.

Warrington, in sharp contrast, had disappointed me with their lack of ambition in the time I was with them, and I couldn't see any improvement on the horizon.

All I had to do was weather the ballyhoo about being the first league outcast to be welcomed back to union and everything would be fine. My last thought before going to sleep was that perhaps there wouldn't be as much fuss as I feared.

I'd hardly got out of bed next morning when the doorbell rang. It was an ITN camera crew. The merry-go-round was not to stop spinning for weeks.

I had trained the previous night with Warrington, little thinking it was my last session with the lads, and was expecting to play in a league match at home to Halifax on the Wednesday night. The club telephoned to ask if I would play in this final game so that I could make a farewell appearance in front of the Warrington fans.

Gareth had already told me that Cardiff were keen for me to play against Aberavon in a Heineken League match at the Arms Park that weekend and were hoping for a bumper gate and to sell the game to television. So, much as I would have loved to experience one last run-out with the team in front of the Wilderspool supporters, I couldn't really take the risk of getting injured.

My sadness at leaving the Warrington fans and all my teammates was, unfortunately, not matched by the feelings I had about leaving the club. I was annoyed by the way Warrington officials had behaved during the transfer negotiations. They hadn't paid a penny when they got me from Widnes, yet they acted as if they'd created me, as if they had a divine right to direct my future.

They opened my letters, threatened to sue me for breach of contract and generally acted as if I was a prisoner trying to escape. After all those years of rugby league criticizing union for their treatment of players who wanted to change codes, at the first opportunity they proved to have an equal capacity for pig-head-edness.

At least I managed to avoid an auction. As soon as it became apparent that a gangway back into union was opening up, a number of clubs contacted me with offers. The highest came from Harlequins, who offered me a contract worth over £100,000. It was a very attractive proposition, but if I was going to leave league Cardiff was the ideal base for me to pursue an alternative career.

Both Swansea and Llanelli were interested, and either club would have been very attractive to me and taken the family a lot nearer to our roots. But there was no chance they could put together the jobs package and transfer fee that Cardiff were assembling, so I pleaded with them to drop their approaches. Had they made their interest official, I suspect that Warrington would have had a field-day playing one off against the other.

This may seem very sly of me, but at that time I thought my chances of moving back were, in any case, exceedingly slim. Hundreds of Welsh players who had taken what some still like to call the traitor's path to the north would have nursed some secret hope of finishing their careers in the game of their boyhood. It had been a forlorn dream for them and, apart from a few weak periods of wistfulness, it was one I was determined not to waste any hopes on. The most I'd ever hoped for was to play a few social games for my village team at Trimsaran before I hung up my boots for ever.

When it became obvious that rugby union's fight against professionalism was a losing battle, there were grounds for more optimism, but up until the moment that Gareth rang to tell me the deal was on I had kept an open mind. I wanted to go to Cardiff for reasons I've already stated, but I also had it in me to pack in playing altogether if Warrington persisted in their awkward attitude.

I joined them only because Widnes could no longer afford the wages they had contracted to pay me. I shall elaborate later on the tragedy of Widnes, but they desperately needed to unload me from their pay-roll. Without a transfer fee involved, several clubs were interested. Wakefield Trinity and Castleford were particularly keen, and I was very tempted by what they had to offer.

When Warrington entered the scene, however, there was no other choice for me. They agreed to take over my contract and, since they were just a few miles down the road, I wouldn't need to move house or change schools for the kids. But there couldn't have been a more traumatic move from one club to another. The first thing I'd learned when I joined Widnes was that our deadliest enemies were Warrington. It wasn't my fault I had to do it, but there are fans in Widnes who will never forgive me. As I ran out of the tunnel on my first game back there I received a volley of spit.

I can assure them that it was never my idea. I didn't even go there on identical terms. Warrington agreed to pay me the same money, but whereas my contract at Widnes involved nothing else but playing rugby, at Wilderspool my duties also included working for the company owned by their chairman, Peter Higham.

I might not have been a willing party at first, but no one could accuse me of not giving Warrington every scrap of my ability and effort. In my first season, 1993–94, I made 30 appearances, scored 293 points and won the game's top two individual awards – the Man of Steel and the First Division Player of the Year award. Only one other player, Ken Kelly in 1981, had ever brought those awards to the club.

In that same season we shared the top spot in the league with Wigan and Bradford, losing the title only on goal average. We had great team spirit, trained hard and enjoyed ourselves. Although we had an excellent team, we needed more strength in depth and I was promised we would get it. The promise was not kept. The following season I scored 292 points, one point less than the previous season's total, from only 29 appearances, and we dropped to sixth position.

Before the World Cup interrupted the 1995–96 season, I scored 77 points in eight games, but it was already obvious that the team weren't going anywhere. I believe I kept my end of the bargain with Warrington. I don't think they kept theirs.

Before I went off to join the Welsh squad in preparation for the World Cup, I spoke to Peter Higham about Cardiff's interest and my desire to do something about my future career. He said that if any clubs, league or union, wanted to sign me they would have to negotiate a transfer fee.

I told Cardiff the situation and then resolved to put it at the back of my mind in order to concentrate on our tough World Cup qualifying group games against France and Western Samoa, which were to take place in Cardiff and Swansea.

The pressures of the tournament and our determination to give Wales something to cheer about meant that it wasn't difficult to forget everything else – even the fact that Gareth was having a torrid time trying to negotiate with his opposite number. Then, in the middle of all this, one newspaper ran a story saying that the deal had been done and that I was on my way to Cardiff.

I went absolutely berserk with the reporter who wrote it. I've fallen out with pressmen before but never as violently as that. The infuriating part was that the report was not only untrue, it came at a delicate stage of the negotiations and gave extra ammunition to Warrington.

Even worse, as far as I was concerned, was the entirely wrong message it sent out to my colleagues in the Welsh squad and all the new fans we had gained. Here was the Welsh rugby team on the brink of their greatest ever achievement and the captain was busy organizing his future in another code.

Thankfully, the boys knew better. We were training and playing so hard there was no doubting anyone's commitment. After beating France at Cardiff we faced the qualifying clincher against Western Samoa at Swansea. The Samoans contained the former All Black giant Va'aiga Tuigamala and were rated a team well capable of dumping us out of the tournament.

The night we played them at the Vetch Field in Swansea will go down as one of the most demanding, physically and emotionally, of my career. The Welsh rugby union team had won the wooden spoon earlier that year, and the country's long lack of success in that direction had left a vacuum we could fill. The media made much of the fact that several of the league side would have walked into the union team.

Had we been able to play at the National Stadium in Cardiff, we might have had a full house. But although we were on the eve of the barriers being torn down, the WRU wouldn't grant us the use of the stadium. Many people were thus deprived of the chance of seeming a momentous game in the flesh, but the 11,000 who crammed into the Vetch that night created an atmosphere that even the Arms Park would have struggled to equal.

Max Boyce said afterwards that it was the first time in ages he'd heard his song 'Hymns and Arias' sung spontaneously by a Welsh crowd. And since it was televised live on BBC Wales hundreds of thousands – including a lot of league fans in Cheshire and Lancashire who can receive the Welsh signal – were able to see it.

My son, Scott, was the official Welsh mascot for the game and stood in line with us opposite the Samoan team during the formalities. He kept tugging at my shirt during the anthems, saying, 'Dad, dad.'

I kept shushing him up but the tugging got so frantic I finally had to give in.

'What's the matter?' I demanded.

He pointed nervously at our opponents. 'They're very big, aren't they, Dad!' For a seven-year-old he was quite observant.

The speed of play and the intensity of the tackling had to be experienced to be believed. It was everything you'd imagine hand-to-hand combat in real warfare to be like. This wasn't due to any ill-feeling between the sides. The Samoans are so physically hard it is the only way they know how to play, and in Va'aiga Tuigamala they had a typically fearsome competitor. But we were determined not to give up an inch of Welsh soil, and not even Tuigamala could make a dent in that ambition. It was a tremendous game to play in, and our 22–10 victory put us through to a semi-final encounter with England at Old Trafford six days later.

Recovering from that match and preparing to meet the English didn't leave me with much chance to catch up on what was happening in the negotiations between Cardiff and Warrington. Some in the Cardiff camp were becoming so frustrated at the lack of progress that they suggested that I should retire from rugby league, move to Cardiff and play for the club as an amateur. The legal brains among them seemed to think that even if Warrington took us to court, any compensation would be a lot less than Warrington were asking as a transfer fee.

I don't know how far this suggestion would have been taken, and it certainly wasn't my idea. Total retirement was closer to my intentions but, again, I wanted to think about nothing other than beating England that Saturday.

It didn't help to keep me focused when the Friday morning newspapers reported that Warrington were threatening to sue me for breach of contract. I was about to lead my country into undoubtedly the most important rugby league international it had ever faced, and my club were waiting to stick me into court.

It was another great day. An estimated 10,000 Welsh supporters braved the delays on the M6 to be at Old Trafford for a game in which England proved too strong for us. We had beaten them in Cardiff earlier in the year to clinch the European Championship, but the English had the edge on us this time.

When the final whistle sounded, I had a sudden surge of uncontrollable sadness. I have never liked losing, but this was more than just a reaction to one result. We had developed such a close relationship in that squad, and I took my responsibilities as captain so very seriously that the realization that this was the end of our dreams brought a flood of regret.

There is a theory that I sank to my knees knowing that this had been my last rugby league game. I knew nothing of the sort. But I did believe it was the end of one precious part of my life. I had received a large sum of money to sign a contract with the Australian Rugby League and part of that contract stipulated that I should play no more internationals after the World Cup. In effect, that was my last game with the three feathers of Wales on my chest. That was cause enough to keep the tears flowing, apart from the fact that I'd never play with that great bunch of friends again.

At the press conference after the match there was little I could say about my future. Somebody asked me if there was any particular reason I wanted to go back to union.

'Because it's easier,' I said. They thought that was very amusing – any slight against union is very popular up there – but it was little more than a top-of-the-head remark. It did carry a grain of truth, however. You take far fewer hits in union than you do in league. And when a player is in his thirties that is liable to be a serious consideration.

With the World Cup over I was able to fix my mind on the situation at Warrington and, as requested, I reported to the club on Monday 23 October for a meeting with Peter Higham, Graham Armstrong and Brian Johnston, the coach.

Prior to the meeting I had popped into the club office to pick up my mail that had been piling up while I'd been away. The girl handed me a large bundle of letters. They had all been opened. They were mostly from fans or charities, asking me to do this or that, but that wasn't the point. They were addressed to me personally and never before at Warrington, or at any of the clubs I'd played for, had my mail been examined. It did not help my mood.

The meeting was more like one of those cross-examinations you see on a TV detective programme. They sat across from me and looked at me as if I had committed some crime. It was all very tense, and the atmosphere wasn't helped when I told them that I felt it was time for me to build a career outside rugby that would last the rest of my life. I would prefer to play out what was left of my career with Cardiff, but if that wasn't possible then perhaps it was time I retired. I told them that I felt they'd had the best out of me and that the physical part of the game was bound to start getting to me sooner or later. I'd given my all and now had the opportunity to rebuild my family's life in Wales and for my children to go to Welsh schools.

Sympathetic was not the word to describe their reaction to my heart-rending speech. My contract had to be honoured, they said, and the only way I could leave was if someone offered to pay a lot of money for my services. Peter Higham did concede that if I wanted to go home and play local rugby for Trimsaran they would be persuaded to let me go.

Meanwhile, Brian Johnston wanted me to go straight back into training. I knew that most of my colleagues in the Welsh squad were being given the week off to get over all the aches and pains left by the World Cup, so I was adamant that I needed a rest, especially with all these negotiations hanging over me.

They agreed and we parted, if not amicably at least aware of where we stood. I assured them I would report for training the following Monday.

'By the way,' I said to Armstrong, determined to have the last word, 'I prefer to open my own mail.'

The following day was my 33rd birthday and we headed for West Wales with the children. I'd told Karen that I didn't feel particularly confident. Cardiff's offer was still nowhere near the lottery-style figure Warrington were dreaming of.

That Saturday was the World Cup Final between England and Australia and I was appearing in the BBC *Grandstand* coverage at Wembley. Afterwards, I went down to the ballroom where everybody who was anybody in rugby league was gathered for an after-match drink. Many made a point of coming up to me, and wishing me luck and saying how pleased they were that I had a chance to go back home and into union. There wasn't a hint that anyone thought I was running out on league. They were all delighted that the walls between the codes were tumbling and that I had a chance to take advantage. I'd been a good ambassador and helped the game's image.

Almost all the Widnes team were there; the players I'd made my league debut among seven years earlier. There was the expected banter, but they all felt I was doing the right thing and were keeping their fingers crossed that it would work out.

We little knew that a multimillionaire called Chris Evans was already putting into place the financial assistance to break the deadlock. On Sunday evening Gareth Davies tipped me the wink that there was a new development, but I'd heard it all before so my hopes refused to rise.

I reported as promised to Wilderspool on Monday and trained as usual. Afterwards I said goodnight to the lads, little thinking it was my final appearance as one of their team-mates.

CHAPTER 3

Cold Cardiff Comeback

The press could hardly ignore the historical significance of the deal that took Jonathan Davies home. Accordingly, the headlines were full of the 'Second Coming', the 'Return of the Messiah' and 'King John back to regain his Throne'.

There were, however, other happenings that in the long run would be a more telling commentary on the profound changes sweeping through the game of rugby. For instance, England's outside half Rob Andrew, Jonathan's deadly international rival in their early days, had just been forced into retirement from the England team whose glory had owed so much to his points-scoring ability.

A month before Jonathan's transfer, Andrew left Wasps to join Newcastle as Director of Rugby for a reported £150,000 a year. Backed by Sir John Hall, owner of Newcastle United, the club formerly known as Gosforth was being swiftly strengthened to take full advantage of the new professionalism. Andrew had been allocated ample funds to buy players and responded by signing up a few of his colleagues at Wasps. Understandably, the London club were not happy at their team being dismantled by their departing star and refused to select him any more, although he was technically still their player for another 180 days.

Effectively ruled out of the first-class game, Andrew felt he had no option but to retire from the England team. Only three months before, Andrew had been deliriously hailed as the hero of England's victory over Australia in the Rugby World Cup in South Africa. With the scores level and over two minutes of injury time already played, Andrew dropped a soaring drop-goal from fully 40 yards to send England into the semi-finals.

It was probably the most famous drop-goal of all time, but within a few months its architect was bound for obscurity; rich obscurity, perhaps, but it was nevertheless a vivid example of what had suddenly happened to the game.

And while one of amateurism's favourite sons was fleeing northwards for the loot, one of its arch-betrayers was making the reverse journey to an excited welcome.

In this bewildering context it was hardly surprising that, happy as he was to be going home, Jonathan had a flood of confused thoughts coursing through his mind. The most uncomfortable feeling was that it was all too reminiscent of his move to Widnes seven years earlier. He still talks with a shudder about the media avalanche he encountered during his first ten days as a rugby league player. It was so intense that the Widnes coach Doug Laughton, who pulled off league's most spectacular signing coup, was moved to comment: 'If I had known we were in for all this fuss and disruption I might not have bothered to sign him.'

Reluctantly facing up to a similar barrage of ballyhoo on his unexpected return, Jonathan found it difficult not to be over-whelmed by the crescendo of voices hyping up his reappearance in the union ranks. Even Doug Laughton joined in by saying: 'With his kind of magic, he'll walk through rugby union. We've certainly had his best years in league but, with his special talent, nothing's impossible. He doesn't owe us a thing.'

Jonathan wasn't feeling very magical but he was grateful he was leaving behind no feeling that he had run out on league. He had hundreds of letters from fans about his departure and, without exception, they all wished him well. Even Warrington felt able to offer a fond farewell. Despite the club having given the impression that Cardiff were stealing him, chairman Peter Higham said: 'We are happy with the deal. We have had a couple of very good years out of Jonathan, who is one of the best players to come north, if not the best.'

The sincerity of his send-off was not, in every case, matched by the warmth of the welcome awaiting him. Cardiff supporters rang to complain about the game against Aberavon being switched from Saturday to Sunday in order for it to be televised live on BBC Wales. Others wrote to the local press protesting at such fuss over a player who had let Wales down by going north.

Jonathan felt better able to cope with that reaction than with those well-meaning people who were already promoting him to the Welsh team – as captain. It was this high level of expectation that corroded the pleasure of his return. He startled his press conference on the Thursday by saying: 'This is another challenge I don't particularly need.'

One or two newspapermen took it as a curious reaction to the fulfilment of his dreams. But he was merely giving a typically honest reaction. More than anything, he was tired. To be confronted with a situation from the wilder reaches of his imagination was very exciting, but the realization of his hopes brought demands in its wake. Many players who had taken part in the World Cup complained of prolonged fatigue in the succeeding weeks. Jonathan had led his country through three of the tournament's toughest matches and the experience had left him drained. He was now being asked to add to that burden the sudden need to prove himself in entirely new surroundings and under a media glare whose potency he well remembered.

He had also just turned 33 years of age. This was a landmark about which he was to be frequently reminded in subsequent months, but the more debilitating period of time was not the 33 years he'd been alive but the 15 months he'd been playing non-stop rugby at the highest level.

He would never admit it publicly, but his big moment caught him at a very low ebb.

There was a clue to his mental state at that time in a telephone conversation I had with him on his 33rd birthday on 24 October 1995, when the deal was dragging on interminably. It so happens that my birthday is two days after his. It was the day I became 60.

We were discussing the various frustrations of the moment when I suddenly remembered: 'By the way,' I said, 'happy birthday,' adding, 'I wish I was 33.'

There was a reflective pause and then he replied quietly: 'I wish I was 60.'

Nor was it true that he and Karen were so homesick that they were desperate to take the first opportunity to return to Wales. They were reluctant to leave.

'We were apprehensive about coming back,' recalled Karen. 'We always planned to return to Wales one day but we were in no hurry. We had created a lovely life in Widnes and we had excellent neighbours. Anne and Mike and their children, Natalie and

Michele, were like an extension of our family. The day we left every one of us was in tears, Jonathan included.

'It was much harder leaving Widnes than it was going up there in the first place. Rugby players are not the centre of attraction as much as they are in Wales and you could go out and not feel you were in a goldfish bowl. We had loads of friends outside rugby and it was a super place to live.

'Having said that, we have settled very quickly in Cardiff, and Scott went to a Welsh school where he soon picked up the language. Welsh is the language of the home again, which is important to us. And the people have been so friendly and helpful, the sadness of moving soon became bearable.'

I sat in a corner of the Cardiff dressing-room and felt very much alone. The room was packed with players, coaches, physios, even the press, and yet I seemed to be isolated. It was a feeling I remembered distinctly from seven years earlier, when I sat in the rather more dingy surroundings of the Widnes dressing-room waiting to step on to a rugby league pitch for the first time.

On both occasions a little bit of sporting history was being made, and the players around me were not exactly delirious with joy about it. When I went to Widnes for a fee that was then a world record, they were the best and most attractive team in the country and it was quite clear they didn't feel in dire need of an expensive new colleague who had never played their game before.

When I came to Cardiff they were on top of the Heineken League and looking capable of dominating the Welsh season, and they didn't seem to rejoice in my arrival either. Indeed, I got the distinct impression that some of them were really pissed off that I was being welcomed back like a long-lost son. I was to discover later that they weren't the only ones who resented my return. But all this took a while to sink in, because in those first two weeks at Cardiff I was in too much of a daze to focus on anything.

Looking back, I believe it was a mistake for me to rush into action straight away but, commercially, it was unavoidable. I'd had only a brief chat with Alex Evans and Terry Holmes and, apart from the players I'd known previously, I had barely exchanged a word with the rest of the team. A longer period of acclimatization might have revealed to me that although the top brass of the Cardiff club had moved heaven and earth to get me, the coaching and playing staff were unconvinced of the necessity. It never even crossed my mind that they wouldn't want to make the most of what I could bring to the team. They were a good bunch of lads and that's all that seemed to matter at the time.

That is the precise point where the comparison with my arrival in rugby league ended. The Widnes players might not have recognized the need to sign me, but once I was there they were keen to see what I could do for the team. They protected me as much as they could and if I didn't get a pass I was expecting it was because they felt I might cock it up. Generally, however, they wanted to see if what I had to offer would help the cause. No other consideration came into it but the eventual success of the team.

That was not the impression I received from some Cardiff players at the outset. Unaware that I was facing any such problem, I was only too happy to get a game under my belt so that I could get over the awkward transition period as soon as possible. The club were obviously anxious, too, to get my new career under way in order to take advantage of all the publicity my arrival had caused. The more new spectators they could attract, the better.

The closer the kick-off came, the more I realized that I had underestimated how much pressure would be on me. And I certainly didn't appreciate how much the Rugby League World Cup, in which Wales's interest had ended only two weeks previously, had taken out of me both physically and emotionally.

The trouble with finding yourself in situations no one else has been in before is that you have no idea what to expect. In the past, the tension on such occasions seemed to work in my favour and make my instincts sharper. But everything seemed stacked up against me this time because everyone expected so much.

Cardiff had done a deal with BBC Wales to move their Heineken League match against Aberavon from the Saturday to Sunday afternoon so that it could be shown on television and they'd have a better chance of a big attendance at the Arms Park. What would have been an ordinary club match suddenly became a big media event. This turned out to be the last thing that my new club-mates and I needed.

Many Cardiff fans were annoyed at the switch – and I was on their side. It seems totally trivial now, but one of the few things I didn't like about rugby league was that they played most of their matches on a Sunday. I am a simple soul, and one of the most enjoyable things about playing in my younger days was the Saturday night piss-up and sing-song after the match. Sunday was a day with the family; for resting your bruises, having a drink and an enormous lunch. Going to league ruined all that. It was training on a Saturday morning and an evening spent as far away from a good time as you could get. You could have a lie-in on Sunday morning but only the lightest of lunches. Even if you had the energy left to go out on Sunday evening, the prospect of Monday morning loomed over you.

That my first game back in union should be switched to Sunday was ironic – it was, however, to be the least of my worries. Just sitting there in that dressing-room, with the famous light blue and black Cardiff jersey hanging from the peg above me, was unreal enough. Six months earlier the chances of me being there would have been a million to one. Even six days earlier the meanest bookie in town would have offered big odds against it.

The world was still trying to get used to the fact that rugby union had finally decided to admit professionalism. There was still something unreal about a union club buying a player from a league club and sticking him straight into the team. As the player concerned, I was having more trouble than anyone in coming to terms with it.

Six days earlier I had trained at Warrington for a rugby league game against Halifax, and here I was getting stripped for a rugby union game against Aberavon. No man on earth, not to mention anyone underneath it, had ever made that journey.

There had been much debate about where I would fit in to the Cardiff line-up. I hadn't been bought to fill an obvious weak spot. In his three years at the club, Alex Evans had pieced together an excellent set of backs who fitted in perfectly with his tactical approach.

Before leaving the Welsh game seven years previously I was an outside half, pure and simple. In league, however, I had filled every position in the backs at club level, and for Wales and Great Britain I had played at stand-off, full-back, centre and on the wing. I was hoping the dreaded tag of being a utility player wasn't going to follow me back into union.

Because Mike Rayer, the regular Welsh international full-back before suffering a badly broken leg the previous season, was only just returning to full fitness, it was decided that I should make my debut at full-back. The theory was that this would give me a chance to settle in a position that would give me a little more time to see things developing. This did not cheer up Mike, who wanted to get on with his comeback, and also brought an immediate protest from Chris John, who was Mike's understudy.

I could understand their sensitivity. The game had just entered the professional world and, with wages and bonuses in the offing, players were more intent than ever on keeping their places in the first-team pecking order. But being a pro also means having the best interests of the club at heart and being prepared to fight for your shirt, and I would have been happy to reassure them that I had no designs on the full-back position. It was, however, where the club wanted me to play in that particular match so there was no point in anyone arguing.

Looking back, I should have requested to go straight in at outside half. It was, after all, the only union position I knew anything about. If they'd been worried about how quickly I would adapt, I'd have been just as happy to sit on the bench until Cardiff had established control of the game and then come on as substitute. I just wanted to get the ball into my hands and see if I could create anything.

At the time, however, I was still thinking that my new team-mates had the same curiosity in mind. How naïve can you get? I was in such a whirl about the move and so nervous about stepping back into union at such short notice, that it was some time before I noticed the awkward atmosphere in that dressing-room. That's when I felt like an interloper.

At the best of times, the hours leading up to a game, any game, are not comfortable for me. Although I try to be my chirpy self, my face turns deathly pale and my stomach begins to grind up the gears for a major throw-up.

Despite feeling sick, I tried to make a joke of the fact that there were pockets in the shorts. Rugby league shorts don't have pockets and I wondered what they put in them. I found out later – they're to put your hands in during those long periods during the game when there's nothing to do.

And when I put on the jersey I wasn't very happy at the long sleeves. I asked one of the attendants to cut them off at the elbow. I gather Mike Rayer wasn't best pleased at me mutilating what he regarded as his shirt.

Then came an event that made me feel stranger than ever. Alex Evans gave a team talk that was directly aimed at the other 14 players. 'Think about your own game . . . think about what you're going to do,' he was shouting at them.

Alex had not been involved in my transfer negotiations and I'd only had a brief chat with him since arriving. He had already announced that he was leaving Cardiff a month or so later to take up a coaching appointment in Australia. He had done an excellent job in transforming Cardiff from a struggling side, and it was natural that he and his team would want to emphasize that improvement in his last few games.

I suppose all the hype about my sudden appearance on the scene threatened to overshadow what was an emotional time for them all, and I can understand the way they must have been feeling. Alex, a very nice guy, had been very pleasant and welcoming and had been very complimentary about my game and my approach, but I realized that since I wasn't a member of the team he built he would be more concerned about their immediate prospects.

He told them that the game was about them and not just about me, that no one should want to be the one to make way for me. Mike Rayer certainly didn't want to, and he didn't blame him, said Alex. But they wouldn't keep me out unless they presented themselves like me, 'totally professional, totally dedicated'.

I just sat there with my head down, staring firmly at the floor. Then we went out for a 25-minute warm-up on the pitch and returned to the dressing-room for a final pep-talk. My churning stomach had me dashing for the toilet before everyone was on their feet, running furiously on the spot, pounding their boots on the floor and working themselves into a frazzle.

It wasn't what I'd been used to. In the Welsh rugby league team we'd got ourselves a little psyched up before the World Cup, but normally in league there was little of this team bonding the union clubs go in for. As professionals, I think league players are wrapped up in their own thoughts before a game. Playing for your living in that code makes demands you don't need reminding about, and there doesn't seem to be much call for a communal gee-up.

Just before the Cardiff team went out someone shouted out a welcome to me and wished me good luck. This made me feel a little better; I'd been thinking of asking Aberavon if I could play for them!

They had been expecting a crowd of around 14,000 but only just over half that figure turned up. The kick-off time of 4.00 p.m. on 5 November would have found many fathers on bonfire duty and electing to watch the match live on television. Nevertheless it was 5,000 more than they would have normally expected and, sadly, I fancy most of those who turned up would have been as disappointed as I was.

It was an experience I found totally alien. I expected it to be strange after seven years in league but it was like playing a game I'd never taken part in before. I was dying to contribute, to get really involved, but I felt like a spectator. They should have charged me admission money. In rugby league, when you want the ball you get it; in union you depend more on someone giving it to you.

I had been worried that I would do something daft like getting up from a tackle and heeling the ball which I had nearly done in training. There were moments when I found myself hesitating. For example, when a loose ball appears on the ground in front of you in league you leap on it like it's a bar of gold and stay down there clinging on for dear life, but in union you have to pick it up or kick it. Lying on it will get you penalized. In union, you can kick straight into touch from your own 22, but you can't in league. They may seem simple things, but even a split second of doubt can put you in trouble.

The first time I caught the ball near our line I remembered that I could kick it into touch but promptly sliced it and gained no ground at all. Then I caught a high ball front on to the opposition which is a suicidal thing to do.

In the end, however, it wasn't confusion that bothered me but the fact that I couldn't get into the game. I'd go so far as to say that I found it harder to adjust to union again than it had been for me to get used to league seven years earlier. You forget how technical it is. In league, what you see is what you get. It is hard but straightforward.

It wasn't even the same game I'd left behind. There had been alterations in the rules which I found difficult at first but, most of all, there had been a change of emphasis. The Heineken League hadn't been introduced before I went north and it had brought new pressures on the way rugby is played at club level in Wales.

I had been following the game via television, so I didn't really expect play to be as intensive and continuous as it is in league, but the number of stagnant periods in that Aberavon match amazed me. Aberavon were near the bottom of the division and played spoiling tactics. Cardiff seemed content just to grind it out, and as a result it was a very slow and uninspiring first half.

For almost 20 minutes I didn't touch the ball at all and after the fast and furious action of league it was a very, very strange experience. I appeared on BBC's *Question of Sport* a week or so later, and when David Coleman asked me how my debut had gone I replied that it was the first time in seven years I'd ever been cold during a rugby match. It might have sounded like a flip remark but it was true.

It wasn't as if I didn't try to get more involved, but either I was taking the wrong positions or my new team-mates didn't seem to think I was the best person to pass to. I was moved from full-back to centre when Steve Ford went off injured, but this didn't seem to improve matters. Aberavon's coach Glen Ball had been my team manager at Neath 12 years earlier and he seemed to have instructed his backs to drift across to cover any breaks I made. Perhaps that left gaps the other Cardiff backs felt they could exploit.

At the press conference after the match the rugby writers mischievously asked outside half Adrian Davies if they had planned to use me just as a decoy. He denied this, adding: 'You can't expect him to come in after seven years' absence and immediately run the show.'

The last thing I expected was to run the show. I had been a union player for all of 72 hours, and my hopes were for an outing that would re-introduce me to the game and give me a feel for my new world without making me look a fool. I was certainly not expecting to play a central role and challenge the club's try-scoring record.

I was also conscious of the fact that Evans had urged his team to show how good a side they were. And, in the end, they did that by winning 57–9. I made one decent break that led to a try for Mark Ring, and I provided the final passes that allowed Mike Rayer, who had come on as substitute, to score two tries. I like to think my presence opened up gaps for the others.

But someone in the press box kept count and apparently I touched the ball eight times in the first half and five times in the second. As the score suggests, Cardiff were well on top in the second half, but there were times when I couldn't get within 30 yards of the ball. This may well have been due to my rustiness in positional play, but while they were enjoying so much superiority, my new club-mates could have given me a few more chances to get acclimatized.

Apart from any help they might have given to me, there was also the consideration that the extra 5,000 who had turned up, plus a million watching on television, might have been interested to see how I would shape up.

The crowd had been shouting for me to get some more of the ball. After the assistant came on to the field with the drinks bottle, one fan yelled: 'They're even missing him out with the water.'

When the final whistle went, my first reaction was relief that I had got through it without disaster, but I was bitterly disappointed about my lack of involvement.

When we reached the dressing-room Mark Ring, who'd played very well and scored three tries, sank exhausted on to the bench. Then he looked at me and said: 'You're not even sweating. You could play another game.'

I fought back the temptation to say that if they were like that, I could play another two.

When it was my turn to go into the press conference I was determined not to complain about anything. I just told them I didn't enjoy not being able to contribute more and it had been rather alien to me. I had come directly from a code in which you can get as much of the ball as you want, but it doesn't work like that in union, and I needed more time to adjust not only to the new code but to the style in which Cardiff play.

They tried to draw me on my ambitions to dictate play like I used to in my former union days, but I explained that it wasn't for me to come straight back and start telling players what to do. I had a learning process to go through.

The main lesson was that my fears about the public's expectations being too high were not exaggerated. I was not going to be the instant Messiah and I needed time to settle myself back into the union groove. I realized, however, that the patience I'd asked for was not going to be forthcoming.

Most of the following morning's reports were less than encouraging, but a few of the writers were sympathetic. Under the headline 'Davies Denied Chance to Shine', Steve Bale of the *Independent* wrote: 'If Jonathan Davies is to be the saviour of Welsh rugby . . . he will need the ball, and by design Cardiff appeared to be doing their best to deprive him of it last night.'

The knowledge that my comeback game would be regarded as a failure, despite the obvious difficulties I had faced, weighed heavily on me. Karen and the kids and my parents were watching the game from Peter Thomas's box but what should have been a happy family after-match celebration was more than a bit subdued. Fortunately, there was little time for dwelling on it. We were still living in Widnes and Scott had to be back at school the next morning.

Then followed a week just as hectic as my first. I had duties for my new employers Jewson, plus talks with BBC Wales and the Welsh Rugby Union about the work I would be doing with them. It meant several car trips back and forth along the M5 and M6 before I next pulled on a Cardiff jersey. This was a friendly match against Cambridge University on Friday night and was a fairly low-key affair. Wales were playing Fiji the following day and most of the Cardiff first team were on international duty or having a rest.

At least I was picked to play at outside half, where I immediately felt more comfortable. Although we allowed Cambridge to come back at us late in the game, we won with plenty in hand. I kicked four good conversions and passed well, but it was still a long way short of what you might call a great personal success.

The main problem was that I was still trying to cope with the Cardiff style and with what was required of the modern outside half. I was trying to create impromptu attacking situations when what they were used to was a distinct and more predictable pattern of play. I was throwing out long passes that I considered worthy of being developed, and the recipients were inclined to run the ball back towards the pack to set up another ruck. And when I stood off the ruck waiting for the pass, the scrum-half would be more likely to pass to the hooker who had been standing off on the blind side so that he could charge through and set up another ruck.

I was so bewildered by it all that I hardly noticed a twinge at the base of my stomach. By Sunday it had become a serious ache and ominously similar to a pain I'd had four years previously when I needed a hernia operation. A visit to the club specialist the following day confirmed that a weakness had developed in the wall of the lower abdomen that required immediate surgery. Cardiff agreed that I should have the operation as soon as possible.

It was quite ironic, because Karen had been due to go into hospital the following week for an operation to cure a digestive problem. Because of the move she had already decided to postpone it until after Christmas, which was just as well. We both couldn't have been in hospital, with three kids and a house to move.

It seemed then just another instance of the sportsman's needs being urgent, but not his wife's. It turned out to be a very fortunate decision. When we discovered the true nature of her trouble three months later, we were told that there could have been serious complications had the original operation gone ahead.

So, luckily, I was the one who entered hospital and although these occasions are never to be enjoyed, it was some relief to think that my name would be disappearing from the headlines for a while.

It didn't, of course. 'Have Cardiff wasted their money?' asked one newspaper when news of my operation was announced.

At least I had a breathing space in which to let my thoughts calm down, think about the challenges of my new jobs, and find a house. Fortunately, the Copthorne Hotel in Cardiff gave us full accommodation while we were house-hunting, and the manager Simon Reid and his staff were terrific to us.

Much of the turmoil of the first week of my signing came from having to meet my prospective employers and discuss what exactly my involvement was going to be. Peter Thomas and Gareth Davies had done the preliminary negotiating on my behalf, but I needed to talk to everyone personally and decide what was practical. It soon became apparent that there were more opportunities available than I would have time to take advantage of.

Jewson, the giant building supplies company, whose managing director Alan Peterson is a Cardiff supporter, had been prime movers in the attempts to bring me back. Apart from the contribution Jewson, as the club sponsors, made to the transfer fee, Alan took a personal interest by mapping out a constructive role for me. He wanted not merely to use me as someone to open branches and make personal appearances but to give me a long-term chance to learn business skills that could be developed when I finish playing.

Arthur Emyr, who had taken over as Head of Sport at BBC Wales, also offered me a long contract to work for them on television and radio in Welsh and English. This was another job that involved some specialized training. I had appeared on both television and radio many times, but now I was given the chance to be an interviewer and experience life on the other side of the microphone, which I enjoyed.

Then came talks with the Welsh Rugby Union. Their president Vernon Pugh who, in his capacity as chairman of the International Rugby Board, had done so much to usher in professionalism, wanted to involve players to help develop the game and assist in the marketing of the 1999 World Cup in Wales. I was the first such development officer to be appointed, and it was agreed that I would work a three-day week, starting immediately, at the WRU's new offices at the University of Wales in Cyncoed.

My appointment was not greeted with wild enthusiasm everywhere. I was still trying to come to terms with my lukewarm reception at Cardiff when news began to filter through that there were certain grumbles from West Wales about the WRU giving me a well-paid job. 'What about Ieuan Evans and Robert Jones?' went the cry. They'd remained faithful to Welsh rugby when I deserted it, and the WRU were now rewarding me and ignoring them.

The parochialism that had dogged Welsh rugby for decades had, obviously, not gone away. It was the very fact that I had spent seven years expanding my reputation in a highly professional game both here and in Australia that gave me the experience the WRU wanted to use. I didn't apply for the job, but I was available at exactly the time the Union were putting together a new commercial and playing approach. Other players have been taken on since and no one could deny that the future looked a lot brighter.

Through accepting the Union job I had to reject some very appealing offers from elsewhere. I would have loved to accept them, but I couldn't give them the commitment they deserved.

Mike Hall joked that I was going to become the first rugby player to work a nine-day week. I couldn't do it all, so I confined myself to one day a week for Jewson, two days for the BBC and three days for the WRU. There was also the small matter of my rugby career with Cardiff, who were paying me no more than they were paying anyone else. I had held many jobs previously, from house-painting to the world of finance, but I can honestly say I have never been so busy – all of which added to the bewilderment of our new life.

Thanks to a generous bridging loan from Peter Thomas, we did not have to wait until we had sold our house in Widnes before buying in Cardiff. And we found a house in record time. We were visiting Gareth and Helen Davies in Llandaff when we noticed a 'For Sale' sign next door. We fell in love with the house immediately. The fact that it was 200 yards from the BBC studios, and not much further from the Welsh school we wanted the kids to go to, was a bonus. Thanks to some rapid legal work we had moved in within a month. And just to prove that some of my countrymen were pleased I was coming home, we had a call from Dyfed Removals in Fishguard. They offered to move us from Widnes for nothing!

While all this was going on, the most important effect of my recuperation after the operation was that it acted as a buffer zone between the two codes. The swiftness of my move to Cardiff, less than two weeks after leading Wales against England, meant that I rushed into union with every instinct still tuned into league. This feeling of being a rugby foreigner must have contributed to the strangeness of my first two games.

Although I didn't play for another five or six weeks, I was able to think my way back into a union frame of mind. The further my experiences in league faded into the past, the more confident I became about the change. I still had to get used to the way Cardiff played, but I was no longer afraid of mixing up the two codes while I was on the pitch.

Off the pitch, however, there was one noticeable difference. Had I still been in league I would have returned to action much quicker. They tend not to believe in long rehabilitations up there. This is why I'd anticipated being off less than a month. In fact, within two weeks of the operation I did a little light work.

Weeks earlier, I had promised Dewi Morris I would visit the school he teaches at in Oxfordshire and help out with the coaching. I did some kicking with the boys and felt a twinge around the operation scar. There was no prospect of me doing much kicking when I returned, so I wasn't too bothered, but it did make me a little wary in training.

Cardiff did not seem concerned about a quick return. Alex Evans was now nearing his departure date for Australia, and the European Cup ties were taking precedence over everything else. The team was playing very well and no one was rushing me. It was also a time when Cardiff didn't have many fixtures because of their European commitments, so the chance of a try-out game was slim anyway. I am not sure now whether I should have presented myself more forcefully as fit and ready for action; it might have brought unwanted complications.

One part of my operation that wasn't publicized was that I took the opportunity, while under the anaesthetic, to have a vasectomy. It left me more uncomfortable than the hernia op, and when I went up to the BBC studios in London the following week to record the Christmas edition of *Question of Sport*, I was unable to stop myself fidgeting.

David Coleman asked me what the trouble was and Ian Botham announced to the world that I'd 'had the snip'.

Amid the laughter, I expressed the hope that this exchange would be taken out before the show was broadcast. Coleman said to the studio audience: 'I told you all the best bits would end up on the cutting-room floor.'

'That's exactly what the surgeon said to Jonathan,' interrupted Botham.

It was some time before the uproar died down enough for the programme to continue. When it was shown during Christmas week, I was relieved that the cutting-room floor had done its job. By then, the effects of both the hernia and the vasectomy had long worn off, and I felt fit and raring to resume my comeback.

CHAPTER 4

Out of Place

*It was a debate that few in the rugby world could resist joining.
Should Jonathan Davies be ushered straight back into the Welsh
team on his return from league?*

*Some had no doubts at all. Even before he had set foot on Welsh
soil again, let alone a Welsh pitch, he had been not only selected
for the national team but elected its captain. These were, of
course, not official moves but the excited reaction of many
who saw his return as the catalyst in the rescue of Wales from
her sorry and subdued status as a rugby nation.*

*There were others, meanwhile, who would have thrown
themselves off Snowdon before contemplating such a thing. They
would have thought twice about even letting him back into the
country.*

*One of the more illustrious names to enter the argument at an
early stage was J.P.R. Williams, the former Welsh full-back of
legendary fame. Wales were due to play Fiji the week following
Jonathan's transfer, and JPR, then a Welsh selector, made the
controversial statement that much of Wales's problem in recent
years had stemmed from the lack of an outside half.*

*Neil Jenkins, the Pontypridd No. 10 who had done valiant
service for Wales over 30 games with his accurate kicking, was
not JPR's idea of the artist who should occupy that position.
'Neil is a lovely lad who tackles and kicks so well,' he said.
'But the Welsh public want fly-halves who can pass and run
and make beautiful jinking breaks. If Jonathan Davies becomes available in time for the Fijian game I would put him
straight in.'*

*Thus was ignited a controversy that was burning brightly well
before the player had made his debut for Cardiff. John Dawes, the
former Wales and British Lions captain, predicted: 'Jonathan will*

justify his place on merit. He'll need a little time to get back into the union mode, but a player of his class will be invaluable in helping develop the youngsters in the Welsh team. It would be silly not to make use of him.'

The verbal exchanges were not confined to Welshmen. Many felt justified in adding their two pennyworth. I feel that Fran Cotton, the fearsome former England forward, summed it up with the loaded comment: 'It is sad that a great rugby nation like Wales should think a 33-year-old former rugby league player their Messiah.'

On balance, Jonathan tended towards the Fran Cotton school of philosophical thought on the subject. Deep down he was highly flattered by the confidence such greats as JPR and Dawes had expressed in him and, if you staked him to the ground under a merciless sun, he might eventually confess that he quite fancied his chances back in the Welsh shirt. But optimism doesn't come naturally to him, and he brushed aside talk of international rugby because he knew he had much to prove both to himself and to Welsh rugby.

Despite his protests, the argument continued even while he was recovering from his hernia operation. David Campese, Australia's star winger, put himself firmly in the bring-back-Jonathan camp, but Wayne Shelford, the former captain of the All Blacks, was just as solidly against: 'It would be a waste of time because you would be stopping the development of younger players,' he argued.

In the end, both sides of the arguments proved futile. Events conspired to deny the hopes of all those who wanted to see his rapid return to the red shirt, and to present him with a far more basic struggle to express himself a reborn union player.

Had things turned out a little more kindly for me, I am certain I could have done a good job for Wales at outside half in the 1996 Five Nations Championship. I would have been the right man at the right time to help the new coach Kevin Bowring impose his brave new pattern of play on the Welsh team. As it happened, he did very well without my help and I wouldn't dream of claiming that Wales would have fared any better had I been in the team. But I would have loved to have had the chance.

I might not have given that impression when I first came back, but my attitude then was clouded by the reception my transfer received. People, respected judges among them, called for my immediate recall to the Welsh team. In a way I was flattered, but mostly I was very annoyed.

I still have a clear memory of the events leading up to my departure seven years earlier. I had captained Wales against Romania in December 1988 and we were beaten 9–15 in front of 17,000 spectators at an Arms Park that was devoid of atmosphere and contributed to the misery of the experience.

It was a humiliating defeat and I acknowledged that I hadn't played well. The fact that the team selection had been ridiculous – Paul Thorburn and Bleddyn Bowen had been inexplicably left out and I felt the wrong set of forwards had been chosen – and that we'd had no pre-match discussions about tactics, which is unthinkable these days, was conveniently forgotten. Within a few days everyone, from the WRU to the Welsh public at large, had convinced themselves that the defeat was all my fault. When I turned up at the next squad session and was totally ignored by all the officials, I was reduced to the state of mind that made me easy prey for Doug Laughton of Widnes a few days later.

Many reasons have been put forward for my defection to rugby league, but the way the WRU and the Welsh fans were happy to heap the entire burden on my shoulders was certainly one of them. They couldn't have contributed to my departure more if they had taken my suitcases down to Chepstow and dropped them over the border.

That, you may say, is all water under the bridge. But I've been called a Judas so many times since then that I find it hard to stomach the fact that the same people who bayed for my blood after that Romania defeat were now calling for me to be reinstated in the team seven years later.

What hurt most was that the lesson hadn't been learned. It was the system not the players that had been wrong. Neil Jenkins had been one of the team's only plus factors, with the value of his kicking, and they were happy to ditch him in favour of someone they'd ditched ages before. It seemed nonsense to me, and I wanted no part of it until I was certain I would have an even chance of succeeding.

Cliff Morgan once told me that the Welsh hate success or failure. It was best to be moderate. I am passionately proud of being Welsh but I was becoming familiar again with this flaw of ours. If people would only get behind Welsh sport and give it more encouragement, I am sure we would achieve far more.

Had I known that soon after my arrival home there would be a new coaching set-up and a fresh approach to the game that matched my own, my attitude at the start would have been different. But when I first came back there was no prospect of any improvement. Wales had won the wooden spoon in the 1995 championships, and their prospects in 1996 didn't look any brighter.

So if I had played in the opening match against England at Twickenham, and Wales had been beaten, guess whose fault it would have been! I was still scarred by the Romanian memory – I didn't fancy ending my career on another suicide mission.

In any case, it was not for me to pick myself for Wales, demand to be captain and dictate what tactics to play. These decisions were for others to make. All I could do was concentrate on succeeding at club level and trust that Wales would want to make use of me; but when your club is loath to give you a chance in your best position you can hardly expect your country to do so.

The shame was that by the time the England match came it seemed to me that Kevin Bowring was on the right track and I would have loved to be in his team. Unfortunately, I was unable to prove to him that I was worthy of the chance. Under better circumstances I might have solved a problem for him.

Wales played Fiji the week after I made my Cardiff debut against Aberavon, and my best friend wouldn't have picked me on that evidence. The next match, Bowring's first as the new coach, was against Italy on 16 January, and while I was still recovering from my hernia operation Neil Jenkins broke his collar bone. There was a vacancy at outside half and Bowring needed an experienced player who could make a positive and adventurous contribution to the more expansive game he planned. I could have been that man, but when was I going to get a chance to show him?

Cardiff, meanwhile, were making impressive progress in the European Cup. In the qualifying group matches, they had drawn with Bègles in France and had been far too strong for Ulster at the Arms Park. This put them into the semi-finals, in which they had to travel to play Leinster in Ireland.

By this time I had been out of action for six or seven weeks. I could have made an earlier comeback but there hadn't been an opportunity. There wasn't a reserve team in which to have a run-out, and first-team fixtures had been postponed to allow them to concentrate on the European matches. It was a frustrating time, and although they selected me as a substitute for the Leinster match I fancy this was just to make me feel involved. After being out of action for so long I didn't really expect to get on unless there was a dire emergency.

Despite shocking weather, Cardiff won well without any sign that my presence was necessary. We were through to the final against the French champions Toulouse at the National Stadium a week later and, again, I was on the substitutes bench. I could hardly complain. It was now over seven weeks since I had played and, in any case, the team that had played so well to get to the final certainly didn't deserve to be disrupted by a 33-year-old whose experience of rugby union in the previous seven years amounted to 160 unspectacular minutes.

The final was an excellent game and ensured that the inaugural European Cup was launched in a manner that would guarantee its future. Unfortunately, it was not Cardiff's destiny to be the first winners. Considering the relative strengths of the two countries at international level at that time, it was not surprising that the French ended as the stronger. But the fact that an exciting game had to go into extra time before being settled was proof of how close it was.

There was a harsh lesson, however, to be learned by Cardiff. In the first half, Toulouse set up an early lead after some blistering work by their backs. It was only through sheer determination and powerful forward play that Cardiff fought their way back into the game to trail 6–12 at half-time. It could have been a lot worse, and when I was sent on to replace Mark Ring at inside centre after the interval, I thought we still had a chance.

Inside centre is not a position I was familiar with. They call it second five-eighth in some countries; a sort of extra outside half who can do a bit of play-making. But Toulouse were a little too quick to allow me any leeway. The first pass I got arrived in my hands about half a second before a pair of bulky French arms were about to enfold me. My next chance was a pass low enough for me to fly-kick ahead. I might have caught it as it crossed the line had I not been impeded by a large French leg.

Thereafter followed a hard scrap in which I made one tackle I was proud of but was generally frustrated by some quick opposing backs. I am grateful to the ITV commentator John Taylor, who said: 'He can't make magic from nothing.'

Outside half Adrian Davies kept us in the game by kicking a 40-yard penalty in the final minute of normal time to tie the match. But Toulouse came back in extra time to win 21–18, and no one can say they didn't deserve it.

It was a game I was happy to be part of and even though I didn't achieve much I felt fit and comfortable which, after my lay-off, cheered me up considerably. When I was chosen at outside half in what was a weakened team to play a friendly at Treorchy the following Saturday, I felt quite happy.

Then I read a small article in the *Daily Express* written by Barry John that was like a blow to the solar plexus. A few writers had taken the opportunity to criticize my contribution to the Toulouse match, but I put that down to the normal ignorance. I could hardly ignore the man regarded as the greatest fly-half ever to play the game.

Under the heading 'Davies comes up short of the mark', Barry said that after two and a half games I was causing many questions to be asked, like 'Has the magic dimmed?' and 'Where does he play?' He went on to say of the Toulouse match: 'He produced one magnificent try-saving tackle to keep Cardiff in the game, but Davies still has a lot more acclimatization to do in the modern union game.'

Even a player of Barry's class might have needed more acclimatization time than two and a half games, especially after being out of action for seven weeks in between the first two and the half. It was another indication of how unrealistic the level of expectation was even among the experts.

What further upset me was that in all the discussion of my limitations, the clear lesson of the Toulouse game was being overlooked. Cardiff were beaten because the French forwards gave the ball out quickly and their backs displayed a speed of thought and action that Cardiff found difficult to handle. In the first 20 minutes, Toulouse produced superb moves to score two tries and looked good enough to rip us apart. It was only a monumental effort by the forwards that brought Cardiff back into the game and made such a close finish out of it.

The result did not hide the fact that the strength which made Cardiff dominant in domestic competition was not going to be enough to answer the big challenges outside Wales. And since the newly formed European Cup was now installed as one of the few potential sources of high income for the club, it was obvious that we were going to have to smarten up at the back. And we had no chance of doing that without much quicker ball from the pack and more adventure from the half-backs.

When I played union before, much was left to the judgement of the outside half. When he received the ball he would decide whether the circumstances required him to kick, pass or run. He was the hub of the team. But playing for league points had brought a less liberal attitude.

Alex Evans had turned Cardiff into a formidable side in which the forwards, especially the back row, were the important influence, both physically and mentally, on the way the team played. Since he is an Australian, it was no surprise that he should introduce typically Australian tactics. They have been very successful for the Aussies and they proved to be very effective at Cardiff in the context of the Heineken League. Despite the fact that Cardiff had excellent backs, the club's strategic philosophy was based on the forwards being the power source. The backs were encouraged not to stray too far and to remain plugged into the mains.

This was an approach favoured generally in Wales. The freedom I had once enjoyed to use my instincts – even the redoubtable Brian Thomas at Neath allowed me my head – was no longer smiled upon. It is small wonder that the traditional Welsh fly-half, the will-o'-the-wisp with the magical side-step, had become a ghost of the past. His place in the game had been overtaken by other priorities, and who could blame coaches for adopting a more controlled approach when they'd seen England dominate the Five Nations with it?

At Cardiff, Alex Evans had taken a team low on morale and self-belief and transformed them into the best in Wales. Under his guidance a lot of players matured and developed individually. There was no better example of this than Jonathan Humphries, who was not recognized to be a first-class hooker until Evans inspired him into progressing to be not only a mainstay and inspiration to the Welsh pack but the captain of the team. The same applied to Derwyn Jones, who became a major player for club and country under Evans.

But I think there were casualties as well as successes. I regarded Mike Hall as the best centre Wales possessed, but in the Cardiff set-up Mike was urged away from his natural game and encouraged to aim his runs towards an area where he could get support from the pack. It is called running back to strength and, although such a ploy has its place as an option, it is negative as a general rule. My instinct is to find space away from the pack and let them catch you up.

The natural abilities of the Cardiff backs as a whole were suppressed in favour of this forward-based strategy, and the main thing wrong with that for a Welsh team is that sooner or later our natural characteristics will find us out. The Welsh are not a nation of giants. We tend to be small compared to the Aussies, South Africans, New Zealanders, French, English and many others too numerous to mention. If we want to live in that level of company we have to make the most of what we've got; and what we've got is speed, skill, guile and passion.

A quick rucking game backed by speed of thought and execution is our only hope and, thankfully, we have a coaching philosophy at international level that has already embarked on this course. This is not meant as a criticism of Alex Evans and what he did for Cardiff, but I think he was right to recognize when his job was done. He accepted a new challenge in his native Australia at a time when Cardiff needed to take the next step forward, to learn to think for themselves. As long as he was there to do their thinking for them, the team would be incapable of developing in the way they needed to.

It was Evans who laid the foundations that took Cardiff to the first European Cup Final at the beginning of 1996. But it was significant that although they performed with great credit against Toulouse, they found themselves up against a team with an extra dimension of attacking flair. It was clear that if Cardiff wanted to make genuine progress in the European game they would have to create that extra dimension themselves. What they had was good enough to get them to the top in Wales but not adequate to meet the vital challenges against foreign opposition.

This was the task that Terry Holmes inherited. I did feel it was something I could help with, but it appeared that the rest of the club didn't agree until later in the season.

There was certainly nothing I could achieve by coming on at half-time against Toulouse in a system that wasn't designed for the quick service I envisaged. I'm not blaming the Cardiff half-backs Andy Moore and Adrian Davies. They were playing to a team pattern that had got them this far but which was suddenly proving inadequate at a higher level.

When the ball did come out to the centres, the French backs had advanced so quickly there was very little time to think of something original and even less space to do it in. I make no excuses for not having a bigger impact on the game, but Cardiff's deficiencies that night were not the fault of any one player – and certainly not the replacement centre.

Those 40 minutes were my only appearance before Kevin Bowring announced the team for the Italy game on 16 January, and although I would secretly have relished the opportunity I could in no way blame him for electing to go with Arwel Thomas, a young outside half who deserved a chance.

Although I was feeling downcast about it all, the Treorchy game the following week offered me a chance to show what I could do in a more familiar role. Even running out on the Oval pitch at Treorchy raised my spirits. I had never been that far up the Rhondda Valley before and I was pleasantly surprised. The surrounding hills that rose steeply on all sides created a typically Welsh scene and reminded me of the pitches I started on down west. There were fewer than 2,000 people in the crowd, the press box was practically empty, and I couldn't see any television cameras. What bliss!

Treorchy fielded what was almost their strongest side, whereas we had lost several players to the Welsh squad who were preparing for the Italy game three days later. The Cardiff side was made up of youngsters, second string players and a few seniors, and I was determined to do what I always used to do in union – start directing operations.

What I wanted was the ball off the top in line-outs – otherwise known as T-ball, i.e. tapped down or caught and immediately fed out instead of pulling it down and starting a drive; channel one ball from the scrum – i.e. the ball travelling immediately from the hooker's heel through the back of the scrum between the No. 8 and the left-hand side wing-forward; and quick service from the rucks, which should be set up centre-field to allow scope for attacking down both flanks.

It was the right thing to do. Treorchy had a strong pack out and although our forwards could have held their own I thought we had the beating of them in the backs. It turned out to be a good open game and they twice took the lead but we put on the pressure towards the end and won 36–19.

It was the first time I had really enjoyed my rugby since returning. It didn't take much; just a lot of involvement, of feeling part of the team, of being in control. It helped that I scored three tries that contained lots of jinking and side-stepping and the odd burst of speed. I also kicked three good conversions, and chipped an accurate cross-kick for winger Steve Ford to score, but what pleased me more than anything was the amount of solid tackling I did. It was far more than the normal ration of an outside half and was an aspect of my league play I was happy to bring back.

Nothing was said afterwards but I didn't need anything more than my own satisfaction. Terry Holmes flashed me a very cheery smile but didn't say a word. I didn't realize how ominous that was. My only regret at the time was that the television cameras, whose absence I'd been pleased at, weren't there to record it all.

The reaction of those newspapers who had bothered to be represented brought a smattering of complimentary headlines.

One read 'Genius Jonathan', which might have been over the top but made a pleasant change. There were many encouraging comments, none more than from the Treorchy camp.

Wales very nearly slipped up against Italy, winning 31–26 after being 31–6 up, but the expansive approach that Wales adopted was like a breath of fresh air and the 21-year-old Arwel Thomas had a very promising debut at No. 10. I have to admit to being envious at the chance he'd had to play in a side committed to playing more adventurous rugby.

The following Saturday, Cardiff were playing at Penarth in the fifth round of the SWALEC Cup and I was intrigued to find out if I was to be given another chance at stand-off. Penarth had long been the butt of jokes in Wales but at this time were doing very well in Division Two of the Heineken League. More than half the team were previous Cardiff players with a point to prove but, the way we had been playing, you couldn't really work up much enthusiasm for their chances.

Cardiff, however, hadn't forgotten their humbling by a local side called St Peters in the same competition two years earlier. Indeed, they had not looked very convincing when beating Penarth's neighbours, Old Penarthians, the previous season. Terry Holmes decided to field his strongest side and, in his opinion, that meant Adrian Davies playing at outside half. Mark Ring had by this time opted to become player-coach of West Hartlepool, so I was put in the centre to partner Mike Hall.

I was upset by this. It has not been my style to go charging into the office to complain about any supposed slight – I was lucky enough not to have had many – but it took a firm bite on my lip not to have a word or two.

I reflected later that I would have been out of order had I thrown a wobbly. Terry had inherited a very good side from Alex Evans and it was important that he kept morale on an even keel. Adrian had done nothing to deserve losing his place and to drop him would have been hardly the demonstration of faith and loyalty that successful teams thrive on. It was not up to Terry to give me the position; it was up to me to make it impossible for him to do otherwise.

That is how I came to terms with it in my mind, but I was becoming tired of making excuses for my treatment. What turned out to be a great afternoon for Cardiff was another bitter experience for me. Cardiff won 62–6 and I needn't have been there. In fact, there were many among the 4,000 who packed the touchlines of the less than majestic Penarth recreation grounds who would have sworn that I wasn't.

Perhaps I shouldn't have played. John Fairclough, the orthopaedic surgeon who examined me the following week, was amazed that I had been able to. He winced when I told him that it was possible because I'd had two pain-killing injections.

My knee had been troublesome since the Treorchy match. Unknown to me, I had tweaked a cartilage in my right knee during the game. I put the pain down to a touch of arthritis and the fact that I had done a bit more kicking of various types than I had for a long time. I had no intention of pulling out of the game and giving the press another chance to have a bitch, so I asked the Doc for a couple of jabs.

This didn't appear to be the normal practice in the Cardiff dressing-room but it was no big deal for me. Before any rugby league game there's usually a long queue for the needle. Unwise, maybe, but a fact of life among the professionals.

Seeing me having injections might have caused some of my team-mates to feel over-protective and to ensure that I wasn't inconvenienced by having anything to do. Whatever the reason, my part in the game was described in one newspaper as 'peripheral', which was a polite way of saying I was hanging around the edges.

Under the circumstances, I had been happy to try to make the most of playing centre but I couldn't do that without the ball. I didn't keep count, but a friend in the stand said I had two passes in the first half, one of which I immediately slipped inside to full-back Mike Rayer in a pre-arranged scissors move, and the other I passed on to Mike Hall.

That was the total of my involvement in a first half in which we raced to 23 points. Despite the fact that the Cardiff backs were running riot and passing movements rippled across the three-quarter line, I was somehow missed out. In the second half I managed to collect the ball from broken play for one decent run and I was given two late conversions to take, but it was all very unsatisfactory.

The Cardiff supporters in Penarth's small grandstand were as disbelieving as I was. 'We know you don't like him, Adrian, but give him a pass,' yelled one.

After missing several kicks at goal, Adrian offered me a conversion attempt from near the touchline. When someone threw me the ball a voice from the crowd shouted: 'That's what the ball looks like, Jonathan.'

I missed that kick, but put one over from right in front of the posts and raised my arms in mock triumph as an ironic cheer went up.

At that stage, I admit, it was easy for me to be paranoid. I was trying desperately to reinstate myself into the game and felt I had achieved a breakthrough at Treorchy, but now I felt as I had done in my debut against Aberavon – on the outside looking in. Some of the newspapers felt the same way. Rob Cole wrote in the *Independent*: 'Jonathan Davies got another game under his belt, yet continued to be largely ignored in what is now being viewed as a back line conspiracy against him.'

The subject wasn't raised among the team and there was nothing untoward in their attitude to me. We had a good drink afterwards to celebrate what was a very efficient and dominating display, and I reflected that perhaps I just wasn't suited to playing centre to an outside half whose game I wasn't familiar with. I did make a suggestion that if I played outside half and Adrian played inside centre we could contribute far more to the team. It was not welcomed but the idea might have gained Adrian a place in the Welsh squad that toured Australia that summer. Despite my obvious problems at Cardiff, my name was still being put forward as a serious contender for the outside-half spot in the Welsh team to play England two weeks later. The Treorchy coach Clive Jones was partly responsible. They had videoed the game for their own purposes and he had sent a copy to Kevin Bowring, suggesting he studied it.

'I would have no hesitation in putting him straight into the Welsh team,' said Clive. 'He can do things that most players in Wales can only dream about.'

On the Sunday evening, I appeared on the *Scrum V* rugby programme and was asked if I thought I would be picked. 'Look,'

I answered, 'I want to play for Wales again but at the moment I am not even playing at outside half for my club.'

As a matter of fact I did get involved with the Welsh squad. I was asked to have a word with Arwel Thomas and go over the video of the Italy game with him. I was delighted to help. He is a very likeable young man and his West Wales background was similar to mine. I also interviewed him on BBC Radio Wales in my new capacity as a media man. I felt very odd interviewing someone who was in effect a rival for the shirt I still coveted.

After the Penarth game, I had become so depressed about the situation that I was on the point of contacting Kevin Bowring and asking him not to include me in the Welsh squad. Then I figured that to do so would sound as if I was presuming I would be in it. As it turned out he didn't pick me but left the door open by saying that he wanted me to get more games under my belt. They were extremely sensible words and I could not have agreed more. Envious I might have been, but I had nothing but best wishes for Arwel and gave him all the advice I could about how to handle the pressures of the Five Nations. I'd made my debut against England 11 years earlier and I wished him as successful an introduction as I had.

What no one knew at the time was that I couldn't have played, anyhow. At training on Tuesday night my knee was hurting so much that Jane Parker, the club physiotherapist, booked me in for a scan at the Cardiff Royal Infirmary later in the week. After seeing the amount of debris floating around the joint, John Fairclough immediately put me on his operation roster and telephoned at 8 a.m. the following morning, which was Saturday, to say that he'd had a cancellation and that I would be his tenth patient that day.

At least someone was happy to put me at No. 10.

CHAPTER 5

Test of Character

A group of rugby writers gathered outside the Cardiff dressing-room in the wide concrete thoroughfare that runs beneath the Arms Park stands. It is a cheerless, echoing place of the type to which pressmen are well accustomed in what seems their ceaseless quest to gather after-match reaction from players.

Cardiff had just beaten Ebbw Vale in a Heineken League match; but only just. With three minutes remaining, Ebbw Vale were leading 13–9 and Cardiff's championship prospects were looking sick. Then Jonathan made a half-break that led to centre Gareth Jones scoring a try that Jonathan converted. Cardiff had sneaked a 16–13 victory they hadn't deserved.

But the waiting journalists were less concerned with the whys and wherefores of an uninspiring rugby match than to collect the thoughts of the player who had been playing his rugby under a burden that had suddenly become public knowledge.

One by one, most of the team had come out of the dressing-room door to scribble their way through the knot of autograph seekers. There was no sign of Jonathan. 'He's probably still in the shower, waiting for someone to pass him the soap,' laughed one of the reporters. The lengths to which his Cardiff colleagues went to avoid giving him the ball was by now a recurring press-box joke but, although there had been other examples of that in the match they had just seen, that wasn't the reason for their slightly awkward presence.

That morning, Saturday 9 March 1996, the Daily Mirror *and* Western Mail *had carried on their front pages the story that Jonathan's wife Karen was suffering from stomach cancer and was receiving chemotherapy treatment. The reports were handled with as much restraint and sympathy as can be assembled when mounting a clear intrusion into someone's privacy, but it was still a shock for Jonathan and Karen to see it in cold print. Luckily, the Davies family were braced for the revelation.*

It had been 19 days since the diagnosis, and they knew the story would come out sooner or later. They hadn't broadcast the fact, but neither had they attempted to keep it a secret. Family, friends, employers and club-mates were all told about the problem. And Karen's appearance with Jonathan at her side at Velindre, Cardiff's renowned cancer hospital, would not have gone unnoticed.

But in the time between the family knowing and the newspapers finally picking up the story, something else had happened that softened the impact. As you would expect in Wales, the family support swung into action immediately. Karen's mother, Vireen, and Jonathan's mother and stepfather, Diana and Ken, were already frequent visitors to the new home at Llandaff, so they merely increased their presence to help tend to the children; uncles and aunties appeared as if by magic; and Jonathan's employers said he could take time off whenever he needed.

The key to the family's ability to cope, however, was provided by Karen herself. Once she had absorbed the shock of being told the nature of the ailment with which she had long been troubled, and had discussed the chemotherapy treatment she had to face, Karen became the calming influence over all those around her.

It was she who restored normality to a household that hadn't seen much of it since the move. All the windows were to be replaced, an extension was being planned, and there were new curtains, carpets, furniture and fireplaces to be selected. Two of her children, Scott, aged eight, and Grace, aged three, had to be ferried to school and nursery, and the baby, Geena, was just beginning to toddle towards the nearest available trouble. Into this Karen had to fit three months of chemotherapy, which involved a ten-hour session at the hospital every three weeks, and to be permanently connected to a bag in between.

It was not an unusual scene at this time for their house to be bulging with people and activity; holes gaped where the windows used to be, fireplaces were hammered into position, men measured for the new extension, while others shredded branches lopped from half a dozen trees – and in the midst of it all Karen remained as bright and as chatty and unflurried as she has always been. Sorrowful visitors went away feeling happily reassured.

Her one regret was that she was unable to watch Jonathan play. Not that it was pleasant watching him try to resurrect his career at that time, but since their teenage days she has rarely missed a game in either code. He didn't feel much like playing and one of his first decisions was to pull out of the Welsh team to play in the Hong Kong Sevens at the end of March. It would have been a good opportunity to wear the red shirt of Wales in a form of rugby which has always brought the best out of him, but there was no question of him allowing himself to be away.

But they agreed that it was important that he continued his battle to succeed at Cardiff, and Karen was determined to watch him as often as possible. Ironically, she was planning to go to the Ebbw Vale game. But after the story of her illness was headline news in the press that morning, it was decided she might have to face the unwelcome attentions of the photographers and so she stayed at home.

'In many ways, my illness has been harder for Jonathan,' Karen said. 'I've had a lot of distractions what with the house and the kids and, in any case, it is easier to cope with when it is happening to you. Had it happened to Jonathan, I'm certain I couldn't have managed.

'When it came out in the newspapers it became even more difficult. What was personal was now public. Relatives and friends are obviously concerned and want to know how you are. That's fine. But when everyone you meet wants to stop and enquire and give you advice it becomes a strain. I can go out on my own and nobody recognizes me. But when I'm with Jonathan people come up all the time. And when he is on his own the same thing happens. People have been very generous with their concern and have the best of intentions, but they don't allow you to put it at the back of your mind.

'It might have been better if things had gone well on the rugby field. But he hasn't had the chance he deserves. He wanted so much to succeed for my sake, but he has found it harder to adjust back in union than he did in league. I remember how difficult it was for him when we first went to Widnes, but everyone at the club helped and encouraged him. That didn't happen at Cardiff, *unfortunately. They say the Welsh thrive on failure, and now I know what they mean.'*

By road from Llandaff, it is 52 miles to Cefneithin, where Karen's mother lives, and another eight down the Gwendraeth Valley to my mother and stepfather's home in Trimsaran. It is a 50-minute journey I'm usually delighted to make; but not this time. It felt like the longest journey I'd ever made, I was so alone and scared.

It was 10.30 on the evening of Wednesday 21 February, and two hours earlier Karen and I had been informed that she was suffering from stomach cancer. I had left her in hospital where she was due to have a laparoscopy to allow doctors to discover the full extent of the illness, to return to a house that was empty because the children were staying down west with their grandmothers.

I called next door to let Gareth and Helen know the outcome of our visit to the hospital, and then headed for the motorway. Late as it was, I had to break the news to our mothers personally. It was the hardest task I've ever had to do; not because the situation was hopeless – it was far from that – but because both families have more reason than most to fear illness. My father, Len, had died at the age of 43 after a long battle against cancer. Karen's father, Byron, suffered kidney failure and although he had a successful transplant he died at 49 of a heart attack while we were all having a meal.

Sharing these experiences has brought us all much closer. My family have always thought the world of Karen. My mother says she couldn't have picked a better wife for me. There is no need for me to dwell on the scenes or the emotions in those two homes when I broke the news. I drove back in the early hours of the following morning so I could be at the hospital first thing. Life had become a nightmare.

It was Karen who calmed everyone down. The doctors had given us every hope but, not unnaturally, we were very worried about how she was taking it. We talk frequently in sport about tests of character: very few of us ever have to face a real one. The mothers brought the children back to Llandaff on the following day, and Vireen and Diana went to visit Karen together. They didn't know what to expect as they approached her bedside, each determined not to appear upset.

2. Proud mother and son after my first cap in 1985.

. Guiding light. Posing with my father as a
hree-year-old.

. Trimsaran Under Elevens in September, 1972. I am in the back row, far left, with Marion Davies,
ront left.

4. Karen and I at a friend's wedding in 1995.

5. Three Angels: Grace, Geena and Scott.

6. Step-father Ken and I recall triumphs on the Trimsaran pitch.

Sharing a trophy with Neath coach Brian Thomas.

Finding my way around Gareth Davies for the Barbarians against Cardiff.

9. Three toffs on tour in Bermuda – me with Mark Ring (left) and Ieuan Evans.

▶ 10. Conniving half-backs, Jonathan Griffiths and I cook up a plot for Llanelli in 1988.

11. Off-loading a pass against France in 1986 despite a burden on my shoulders.

▲ 12. Anxiously sitting alongside Widnes coach Doug Laughton (centre) while I wait to make my rugby league debut against Salford in January 1989.

◀ 13. Delighted Widnes captain holds aloft the Regal Trophy after 24–0 defeat of Leeds in the 1992 final.

14. Flat-out at the Vetch Field, Swansea, to complete a hat-trick of tries for Widnes against Wigan in the 1991 Charity Shield.

15. Interviewed on BBC television's *Grandstand* before the John Player Trophy final at Bolton Wanderers the day after signing for Widnes.

6. My last try for Llanelli on 2 January 1989. Bleddyn Bowen (10) still swears I didn't ground it properly.

7. Wembley here I come! Delight after scoring my second try for Widnes against Leeds in the Challenge semi-final of 1993.

18. Bobby Goulding nearly kills me with a cuddle as we celebrate our victory over Leeds.

19. I manage to get a kick off before Australia's Laurie Daley gets too close.

20. Rugby league's award-winners, 1991: (l to r) John Monie (Wigan), Coach of the Year, Jonathan Davies (Widnes), 1st Division Player of the Year, Paul Schofield (Leeds), Man of Steel, Denis Betts (Wigan), Young Player of the Year, John Holdsworth, Referee of the Year.

But Karen greeted them with the words: 'Right, let's have a good cry now and get it over with. After that, all I want to see are smiles because I'm going to beat this.'

She was so positive about it all that everything was soon back to normal – or as normal as could be. With Karen having to be in and out of hospital for chemotherapy treatment over the next 12 weeks, the mothers worked out a schedule so that one or the other would be staying to help with the kids. The blessing was that we were back in Wales. Had we still been living in Widnes, it would have been far more difficult to cope.

Even with building work, trees to be cut down and curtains and furniture to be bought, life went on pretty much as it had before. Chaotic at times but, then, we're used to that. The main thing was that Karen responded very well to her treatment and, with few side effects, was able to devote her usual attention to the children.

Normality for me, of course, meant playing rugby or attempting to, at least. When Karen's news hit us, I had just got over my knee operation, was back in training and ready to play. Because the international season was at its height, there were very few club fixtures and Cardiff had none in which I could get some match fitness.

While I was cooling my heels, I'd had two pieces of encouragement. Wales had chosen me to play in the Hong Kong Sevens, and the Barbarians had selected me at outside half for the annual Mobbs Memorial match against East Midlands.

I love sevens rugby and going to Hong Kong would give me a chance to test myself in the best of company. As for the Baa-Baas, it was the first time they had chosen a former rugby league player. For over a hundred years anyone who'd played for the Barbarians and subsequently turned professional was automatically expelled. I was the first one to be allowed back, and that made me very proud. The other fact that cheered me up was that they had chosen Robert Jones at scrum-half. To be reunited with my former partner in the Welsh team was the best thing to happen since my return. Suddenly I had two chances to prove myself away from the problems at Cardiff.

Before then, Robert and I had a more immediate date on a rugby pitch. His club, Swansea, had been drawn at home to Cardiff in the sixth round of the SWALEC Cup on Saturday 24 February – three days after we found out about Karen.

I had trained on the Tuesday night and knew that Terry was planning to play me in the centre again. I wasn't happy, but by then I had more important things on my mind. Although we weren't told about Karen's condition until Wednesday I'd been nagged for several days by worries that something was wrong, and the confirmation of it forced all other thoughts out of my mind.

On that sad drive down to Cefneithin, I resolved to take a break from the game and concentrate on Karen. Certainly, I wasn't going to take up the Hong Kong invitation. There was no way I was going to leave the country. I didn't really want to leave the house.

My perspective on life had changed completely. One moment I was engrossed in the battle to re-establish myself as a rugby union player and the next the rest of my rugby career didn't matter one bit compared to seeing Karen get well and the family restored to an even keel.

But in her insistence that our life should be as normal as possible, Karen wanted me to carry on playing. The rest of the family joined her in urging me to play in the Swansea game. On the Thursday night, Terry Holmes took me out for a drink. He felt I should play, too. I wasn't sure. I felt I was so angry with life in general that I might go out there and inflict physical damage – probably on myself.

Any family that has gone through the trauma of an illness will recognize the problem of feeling helpless and not knowing what to do for the best. But I realized that if I wanted to be as positive as Karen then I had to carry on as usual. Besides, Karen has always taken a keen interest in my career. The game was being televised and she wanted to see me playing in it. She has rarely missed an opportunity to watch me play. She was just as determined to see me succeed as I was.

So play I did and, although I didn't have any appetite for it, the game didn't turn out too badly. Cardiff won and I scored a 40-yard drop-goal to help clinch the victory, but there was no deep satisfaction for me. I still wasn't getting involved enough for my liking.

Observers were still making pointed remarks about the service I was getting. The former Welsh full-back, Paul Thorburn, who was part of the television commentary team, said as we were lining up: 'There's not a lot of love lost between Adrian Davies and Jonathan; let's see if he gives him the ball today.'

I tried to dodge inside with the first pass I received but got caught; I then misdirected a pass that led to a Swansea break which Nigel Walker stopped; but I wasn't getting any ball I could work with. When I did get into a promising position, the ball went elsewhere. There was one instance when Adrian gave a reverse pass to Mike Hall when I was open on the other side of him with an overlap.

We already had our noses in front when I got the chance to drop a goal from a long way out on the left that put the victory beyond all doubt. That cheered me up, but there were still many questions to be answered about my lack of involvement.

There had been a lot of needle before the game arising from the fact that when Alex Evans was in charge of Wales a few Cardiff players had taken over places previously occupied by Swansea men. The Cardiff hooker Jonathan Humphries had displaced his Swansea counterpart Garin Jenkins; Hemi Taylor had taken the No. 8 spot from Stuart Davies, and Derwyn Jones had replaced Paul Arnold in the second row.

The tension among the forwards led to some violent confrontations in the first half, but a major flare-up was avoided. Swansea had more than some old rivalries to upset them in the first half. They were denied a penalty try after some tremendous pressure and their outside half, Aled Williams, missed four out of four kickable penalties. They could have had a clear lead before we got into our stride.

I felt sorry for Aled. Anyone can miss kicks, but the fact that he is normally so accurate made it worse. I think it affected his game generally. No offence to Aled, but I found myself wishing I'd been playing outside half for Swansea instead of unwanted centre for Cardiff. I think I could have swung the game.

I wasn't the only one who thought that. The former Wales skipper Brian Price wrote in the *Western Mail* that Swansea had to watch their outside half play badly while Cardiff wasted a better one: 'How galling it must have been for them to see Cardiff playing one of the world's greatest outside halves at centre and then operating what appears to be a form of apartheid towards him. Cardiff appeared to only give him the ball when they knew it would be an embarrassment to him. I wonder for how long Jonathan Davies will take this treatment?'

Although many had commented on the lack of decent ball I was given and suggested that I was deliberately being ignored, I had never made any statement about it. Even to friends I would shrug my shoulders and pass it all off as one of those things. The plain fact was that in the middle of the action these things never occurred to me. I was trying desperately to fit into Cardiff's pattern. The only time I'd felt comfortable was when I was playing outside half and given the freedom to run the show, but even when I was playing centre I desperately wanted to make a genuine contribution. I refused to come to the conclusion that I was being purposely ignored. I must have been doing something wrong, but I couldn't see what.

One thing was certain – I wasn't going to win any sympathy by moaning. The so-called Messiah complaining that he couldn't do miracles because the bad boys wouldn't give him the ball was not an image I fancied. It was up to others to comment on it if they wanted to, but I was saying nothing. I wasn't even certain there was any foundation to it. I certainly felt I wasn't being given any opportunity in a system that would have suited me, but I wasn't prepared to go along with the conspiracy theory.

By now the Five Nations Championship was under way, and although I suffered twinges of regret that I wasn't playing, I had plenty to say about the action. I was appearing on BBC's *Grandstand* during the matches, interviewing players on the radio before and after games and writing a weekly comment article in the *Independent on Sunday*.

When Wales went to Twickenham for their opening match against England on 3 February, I shared the *Grandstand* pundits' spot with Rob Andrew. When I made my Welsh debut in 1985 it was against England and Rob was my opposite number. We had been very keen rivals in the years before I went north, and we could have been facing each other again 11 years after our first encounter. Instead, we were sitting up in the stand studio pontificating like a pair of old codgers. I get on well with him and England will miss him for a long time yet.

The experience was far more uncanny for him. He'd been a fixture in the England team for ten years or more, a hero of the World Cup six months earlier, and suddenly he was out of it. I'd been out of it for seven years.

Strangely enough, the outside halves on the pitch were not all that different from us. England's Paul Grayson is in the Andrew mould but not quite as accurate as a kicker, while Arwel Thomas was a bit like me on his debut – small and cocky. But I doubt if even I would have been as cheeky as he was. The game was only 11 minutes old when he decided to run a penalty within fairly easy kicking distance. I've always prided myself on being bold, but I don't think I would have turned down a chance of putting an early three points on the board. But Arwel took England and all Twickenham completely by surprise. He took a tap penalty and set the ball moving across the Welsh line for Hemi Taylor to crash over for a try.

It gave Wales a terrific start and their adventurous approach to the game brought Kevin Bowring deserved praise. Unfortunately, a drab and negative English team managed to punish Wales for a few mistakes. At least they were mistakes made while trying to be positive. Arwel made some of them but it was a very encouraging performance by him. He'd been given the sort of freedom a succession of Welsh outside halves, Neil Jenkins especially, had only dreamed about, but he had made the most of it. That's the sort of freedom I would have loved at Cardiff.

Against Scotland two weeks later, Wales improved even more, but the Scots, who had made an impressive start to the season, gained a narrow victory 16–14. Wayne Proctor had scored a try in the last minute to give Arwel a chance to give Wales the draw they deserved with the conversion. But from a very difficult angle near the left touchline he curled it just short of the near upright.

But, generally, Arwel had done very well again. If he was let down by anything it was inexperience, but there was every justification for keeping him in for the visit to Ireland two weeks later. My chances of making the team were receding by the minute, but since Karen's illness had been diagnosed the prospects were not uppermost in my mind.

Kevin Bowring had made it clear that I was in his plans but, obviously, he wanted to see me in competitive action in the No. 10 shirt before considering me for the team. He offered me a game for Wales 'A' against Ireland 'A' which was to be played in Dublin on the eve of the main international. But that would have meant two nights away from Karen, so I declined. Cardiff had a friendly against Richmond that night so I settled for that chance to get a match in before I played for the Baa-Baas the following week.

Richmond had recently acquired a millionaire backer and had made a very big offer to Adrian Davies and Andy Moore. It was far above what they were getting from Cardiff and was very difficult to refuse. I'm not sure what sort of team they had out that night but they obviously needed reinforcement. We beat them 82–0 and I enjoyed being at outside half and in control of the proceedings.

For some reason the local press didn't realize the game was on and very few spectators turned up. I was down on the team-sheet as John Davies. It was that sort of night but I didn't care. I just enjoyed myself.

We scored 11 tries and I think I had a hand in most if not all of them. I also kicked 11 out of 11 conversions from all angles. It was very satisfying, particularly as we had two young and very promising centres in Delme Williams and John Calderley who I made sure saw plenty of the ball. Nigel Walker was in his element and it was a super rugby evening. I'm not sure Richmond felt that way. One newspaper suggested they were chasing the wrong Davies.

My reunion with Robert Jones in the colours of the Barbarians the following Wednesday was featured on BBC Wales. Robert and I were the half-backs when Wales last won the Triple Crown in 1988 and it was great fun getting back together. The Barbarians had some good players, including the great English back-row forward Ben Clarke, but we weren't all that well balanced as a team.

East Midlands, as the name might suggest, are usually a side made up of players from various teams in the area. But on this occasion the team consisted of the entire Northampton XV which was annihilating all opposition in the second division of the Courage League and provided not only the English half-backs Paul Grayson and Mark Dawson but also the brilliant Scottish fly-half Gregor Townsend.

As is traditional, the Baa-Baas didn't assemble until just before the game and it took us about 20 minutes to sort ourselves out. By then we were 21 points down. But, although we were outgunned in certain areas, we made a very good game of it. It was like old times playing with Robert and I thoroughly enjoyed it. I kicked well out of my hands, made a couple of decent breaks, set up a try or two and made some very satisfying tackles.

I didn't see any Welsh representative, but one international coach picked me for the Welsh team on the strength of what he'd seen – the trouble was that he was in charge of the Irish team! New Zealander Murray Kidd was coach to the Ireland side who had beaten Wales 30–17 in Dublin the previous Saturday.

Arwel Thomas had been caught early in the match by a merciless Irish rush and, as they say in the game, received a good 'shoeing' which left him very groggy and he didn't play very well. Kevin Bowring was being urged to make changes for the game against France, which was now Wales's only chance to avoid another wooden spoon.

After watching the Barbarians game, Kidd told reporters that if he was picking the Welsh team for France I would be in it. 'I was pleasantly surprised by Jonathan's performance against the East Midlands,' he said. 'If they want to continue the fast open game it would be a good option to bring him in. The thing that impressed me most was his defence. The kids in the Welsh team are playing very well and his experience would help them get even better.'

The debate about who should play at outside half against France was reflected by the *Western Mail*, who ran a poll on the subject. Readers had to decide between Arwel, Neil Jenkins and me and almost 4,000 voted. The result was Neil Jenkins – 1,464 votes; Jonathan Davies – 1,451; Arwel Thomas – 665.

Considering that hardly anyone in Wales had seen me play outside half for over seven years, I did quite well to lose by only 13 votes. The only vote that counted, however, was that of Kevin Bowring, and he chose Neil: a decision I could not fault. I would have loved to play, but Neil had been so unlucky to miss out on the new-look Welsh tactics.

Had he not broken his collar-bone he would have been involved from the outset. He had borne the brunt of several stagnant years when his boot was Wales's only reliable weapon, and he deserved the opportunity to show there was far more variety to his game.

Outside halves live or die by the pattern they are asked to play in. If they are in a struggling team or one that favours a tight, mauling game they have little chance to impress. The latter fate was awaiting me in my next game for Cardiff which was against

Ebbw Vale at the Arms Park that Saturday. Over four months after I had joined them I was to be given my first chance to play outside half in a competitive game.

The day was ruined before it began. That morning's *Daily Mirror* splashed the story of Karen's illness all over the front page. The *Western Mail* also had it on their front page, but the rest of the press played it down or ignored it altogether. Karen and I were upset and annoyed but not surprised. It's par for the course. She was not a film star or a television personality; neither was I for that matter. But she happened to be married to a veteran rugby player and that was enough to turn her problem into a sensation, in the eyes of one paper at least.

We knew the news would get out sooner or later, but it was like reliving the initial impact again. The sad thing was that Karen had been invited to watch the match from Peter Thomas's box, but we felt that the attention of the press might have made it an uncomfortable afternoon for everyone.

In that respect, she was lucky. It was a pretty dire game and Cardiff's performance was rated by one report as 'one of the most jaded and possibly the worst of the season'. At least no one blamed me. I kicked 11 points and hit the post with my other two attempts and I made the half-break that led to Gareth Jones scoring the late try that gave us an undeserved 16–13 victory.

Several of our forwards were still involved in the Five Nations with Wales and were undoubtedly tired, but we took entirely the wrong approach. We put the emphasis on the maul and the scrum, and opposing teams had learned how to deal with it. I couldn't believe how little of the ball I saw.

We had a big crowd that day and they were bored stiff. Gareth Roberts reported in the *Western Mail*: 'Doubtless many turned up in the hope of seeing Jonathan Davies's first league game at fly-half. But just as in previous meaningful encounters when the prodigal one was blatantly ignored or abused by bad distribution so, on this occasion, the trend continued.'

Whether through design or a tactical plan I hadn't been told about, the ball was deliberately kept away from me and the backs. Our pack were once camped near their line and eight or nine scrums took place without the ball being passed out to me. And we were losing at the time. Everyone at the club was so disappointed at the way we played.

I was very dejected. Everyone had been very kind and considerate about Karen, but the one thing that would have cheered her up that day would have been a good performance by her husband, and I was annoyed that I hadn't been able to deliver it. I had a drink and a chat with some of the Ebbw Vale boys after the game and then I took her out for a consolation Chinese meal.

Because of the France game the following Saturday I had another free week. They had offered me the chance to be outside half and captain for Wales 'A' against France 'A', but I didn't really see the point. The Five Nations was as good as over, and I'd already decided I wasn't interested in gaining a place in the Welsh squad to go to Australia, so it was better for a tour candidate to play. Adrian Davies, who had played in the previous Wales 'A' team, was chosen instead but when he pulled out with a knee injury they came back to ask if I would change my mind. Perhaps I should have had a game, but I really did feel it was better to give a youngster a chance to impress and they picked Shaun Connor of Abertillery.

My next appointment in the No. 10 shirt was going to be at my beloved Stradey Park. Adrian's knee was still proving troublesome, so I was to continue at outside half against Llanelli in the quarter-final of the SWALEC Cup. It was a game that had plenty of emotional involvement for me. Llanelli were my boyhood heroes, my father played for them, and although they rejected me as too small when I was a youngster, I played my last season for them before joining rugby league. This was to be my first reappearance there.

Added to all that, my brother-in-law Phil Davies was the Llanelli captain. He and my sister Caroline were due to move to Leeds at the end of the season, where Phil was to become player-coach of Leeds RUFC. He desperately wanted to leave on a high note and that meant leading Llanelli to the SWALEC Cup. Talk about mixed feelings!

But there was no doubting my anxiety for Cardiff to win. My last appearance in the Cup Final was with Llanelli when we won in 1988. Now I wanted to go back with Cardiff and get some satisfaction out of the season.

It was like the old days when we used to live for matches like these. It was odd turning up at Stradey in the Cardiff bus. Swansea were the local rivals, but Cardiff had always been the ogres from the east. Some of them might have forgiven me by now for leaving them to join Widnes, but they would never forgive me for joining Cardiff on my return.

The great Barry John left Llanelli to play for Cardiff in the Sixties. He returned for a match and scored four drop-goals for Cardiff. He was booed off the park and one fan tried to attack him.

My chances of doing the same thing on this occasion were spoilt because I missed two drops in the first half. Good, long kicks they were but they drifted off right, much to the delight of the locals.

It was a hard-fought game rather than a classic and what gave it even more spice for me was that my opposite number in the Llanelli team was Jonathan Griffiths. Jonathan had moved north to join St Helens not long after I went, and returned only a few days after me. While all the hullabaloo was going on about me, he slipped quietly back almost unnoticed.

He'd also found it difficult to command a regular place in the Llanelli team. When he left he was an excellent scrum-half but, like me, hadn't been given an extended chance in his original position. Only a day or two before the match he had been quoted as being sympathetic about my predicament. He was about to make it worse.

Although Cardiff seemed to have the edge in the set-pieces, the service was very slow and Llanelli were much quicker around the field. They gave us a torrid time in the first half but despite all their threats couldn't score a try. With Justin Thomas missing four kickable penalties, we were fortunate to be 3–3 at half-time.

Ieuan Evans scored a try to put them 8–3 ahead, but then our forwards took a grip of the game. After one period of pressure near their line I put a grubber kick through for Nigel Walker. Ieuan managed to get to it, but his kick into touch gained only a yard, and from the line-out Andrew Lewis scored a try that I converted to make it 8–10.

We continued to dominate but our forwards decided to keep the ball in the back row. We were a yard or two from their line and we were screaming for the ball. But scrum followed scrum. Eventually the ball bobbled between Hemi Taylor's legs and popped out for Rupert Moon to snaffle. He passed to Justin Thomas who found touch at the half-way line.

Having been let off the hook, Llanelli counter-attacked and Jonathan Griffiths made two great runs reminiscent of his rugby league days. One of them led to a penalty in front of our posts. Justin Thomas made no mistake and we were beaten 11–10. Llanelli might have deserved to win, but we'd still only been beaten by one point after having all that possession. It was so unprofessional I could have screamed.

All Llanelli were delighted and the headlines next day were of the 'Griffiths wins the Battle of the Jonathans' variety. I didn't begrudge him that. I was delighted that a rugby league man had made the only decent breaks in the game. I was very sad that despite all the praise he got, Jonathan still couldn't keep his place in the team. I knew exactly how he felt.

I just despaired at our tactics. At half-time Terry Holmes had demanded quicker ball and that is exactly what we didn't get. I can take any amount of criticism if I've failed in any way. But I detest being part of something that goes wrong for lack of thought. I was even angrier later when I was made the scapegoat for the defeat.

As for Llanelli, the word Judas had rung around the ground when I was taking a kick. Why I should be singled out for that I can't imagine. It was Phil who was leaving. I'd come home.

However, after I'd drowned my sorrows that night the only thing that left any lasting anger about the game was the mental state of the supporter who, when I was taking a penalty, shouted out: 'How's your wife?'

CHAPTER 6

Benched

Jonathan completed his comeback season sitting on the replacements bench watching Cardiff beat Llanelli 65–13 and still failing to win the Heineken League. For once, the team's frustration matched his own. They had been favourites to win the major trophies that season but after being knocked out of the Cup by one point at Llanelli they had now failed to win the league by two tries.

In an attempt to create an incentive for more open rugby, the League had introduced a bonus system by which a team received an extra point for scoring three tries, two points for five tries and three for seven tries. In the event of two teams finishing with the same number of points, the one scoring the most tries would win. So, despite having won 18 games to Neath's 17 and gaining the same number of points, Cardiff lost because they scored only 119 tries to 121.

The system created a thrilling climax to the season because Neath's final game against Pontypridd and Cardiff's against Llanelli took place at the same time and were shown simultaneously on Welsh television, one in Welsh and the other in English. Neath had taken a superior tries total into the games so their 45–25 victory was enough. Some Cardiff fans complained that if their team hadn't wasted time taking conversions they might have scored the extra tries to win the league.

While the arguments raged about whether this was the true meaning of the game, Jonathan was able to push rugby to the back of his mind with some relief. He was saddened by the way Cardiff had treated him and, having the enthusiast's natural desire to be involved in the action, he hated being on the bench, but if that is where they wanted him he was content to oblige. Seeing him thus humbled would no doubt cheer up some people.

He had been heartened by the number of clubs, both league and union, who had telephoned to express their sorrow at his predicament and to offer him a place in their team. He could have been off to play in shirts of enough different colours to make up a rainbow, but he was determined to stick it out with Cardiff.

There were other things on his mind. He still had his jobs to get on with, for one thing. Far more importantly, Karen's condition had shown welcome improvement after her 12-week course of chemotherapy, but her doctors wanted another 12-week course to consolidate it. And if he wasn't required to play for Cardiff, he could at least help their future recruitment plans. He was dispatched north on a secret mission to talk to three players who had shown interest in returning to Union – Scott Quinnell, Scott Gibbs and David Young. He was also asked by Iestyn Harris, who had taken over his role at Warrington, for advice on how to deal with the many offers he received.

Jonathan's return to play rugby union in Wales had brought confident predictions of a stampede of homecoming exiles from the north. Just as his departure in 1989 had paved the way for a mass exodus of talented Welsh players eager to seek their fortunes in the professional code, so it was imagined that his reverse journey would again see him in the role of Pied Piper.

There was no stampede at first; it was more the pitter-patter of tiny feet. One scrum-half to be exact: Jonathan Griffiths, who had been the star of Llanelli's cup victory over Cardiff. His reward was hardly to get into the side since. Like Jonathan, he was on the bench when Llanelli played Cardiff in the last game of the season.

Another scrum-half, Kevin Ellis, who was only pausing on his way to play league in Australia in the summer, also appeared, but was refused permission to play in Heineken League matches and was confined to the odd friendly for Maesteg and Treorchy.

The only other to arrive was veteran winger Phil Ford, who had already decided to return to his native Cardiff to become a pub landlord after a distinguished league career with Wigan, Bradford and Leeds. The sudden opening of the gangway gave *him the chance to round off his playing days in union. He played for Fourth Division Rumney and guested for his old club Cardiff in a friendly against Pontypool in which he scored a hat-trick of tries.*

The reason why the road to Wales was not clogged immediately by returning defectors was twofold. Firstly, rugby league clubs had just received an £87 million windfall in return for changing to Rupert Murdoch's summer Super League and were able to offer good money and more security to their players. Secondly, union clubs in South Wales had hardly enough to pay the players they already had, let alone undertake the costly repatriation of the exiles, until the promise of lucrative television deals began to materialize as the 1996–97 season approached.

Jonathan's return was possible because forces outside the game both raised his transfer fee and guaranteed his income. Jonathan Griffiths could afford to forgo his league earnings because he was able to restart his career in the Fire Service.

The rest remained where they were at that stage; tempted, perhaps, by the idea of home but tied by contracts or fascinated by the prospects that were opening up in union in England.

Not long after Jonathan arrived back, Cardiff's highly gifted centre Mark Ring left to take a lucrative post as player-coach of West Hartlepool; Jonathan's brother-in-law Phil Davies, captain of Llanelli and a towering presence at Stradey Park, agreed to accept a three-year contract to coach and play for Leeds RUFC; Gareth Llewellyn, the inspirational captain of Neath and a vital member of the Welsh pack, signed for Harlequins, and his brother Glyn for Wasps; Cardiff's half-back pair Adrian Davies and Andy Moore joined Richmond . . .

The list grew week by week and almost every bright young player in Wales seemed to be the subject of an approach by a wealthy English club. The Welsh Rugby Union acted to stem the flow by appointing more players as development officers and offering improved contracts to home-based members of the Welsh team, but clubs were finding themselves hard pressed to get anywhere near the pay being offered across the border.

Few had foreseen that the great dawning of rugby's new world was going to bring with it a threat to the stability of the club scene in Wales. For a century, the only enemy had been rugby league, and its frequent raids had been a constant irritation that the Welsh had managed to survive. Now a new and more dangerous threat was looming. It was the cruellest irony, as English union clubs, many of whom had acquired wealthy backers, could offer better packages in places far more accessible to South Wales than Lancashire and Yorkshire.

Jonathan's attempt to persuade some of his Welsh rugby league team colleagues to follow him to the Arms Park had mixed results. David Young agreed to transfer from Salford; Quinnell agreed personal terms, but then Richmond came in with an offer Wigan couldn't refuse and tempted the player with a reputed £100,000 a year; Gibbs also agreed to join Cardiff, but the transfer fee St Helens were demanding was a sticking point and he was fined eventually by Swansea for a reported £200,000.

It is significant that all three insisted that they wouldn't join Cardiff unless Jonathan guaranteed he was going to be there. They'd heard about his problems. 'They're just jealous,' they said.

When the 1995–96 season came to an end on 15 May, it marked my completion of precisely 21 months and two weeks of continuous rugby involvement interrupted only by a couple of surgeons. It had been an amazing period of my life, as it would have been of anyone's life, but I wasn't sorry to see the back of it. Mentally, I was exhausted, because there had been an awful lot of emotion and anguish bound up in it.

Obviously, the final six months were dreadful. From the rugby point of view, it was an extremely low point. I'd had many disappointments in my early days and when I first began in league, but nothing to compare with the frustration and humiliation of the last few months of the season.

I tried to comfort myself by looking back over the whole period. There may be one or two players who can point to similar lengthy stints, but I can safely claim that no other would have packed as much variety into that time as I did – playing for two rugby league clubs and a rugby union club, being Man of the Match for Great Britain against Australia, calling at Buckingham Palace to pick up an MBE, spending the summer playing in Australia, captaining Wales to the semi-final of the World Rugby League Cup, playing for the Barbarians and wearing out a hole on the Cardiff replacements bench.

It was in that final position that I rounded off this unique period in the annals of rugby achievement. If nothing else, it proved that life can contain humiliations as well as honours. They are not usually strung so closely together, but if you accept the highs you have to tolerate the lows. I imagine that some players in my position would have refused to sit on the bench, or faked an injury, but I belonged to that club and if that's where they wanted me that's where I would be. It might have cheered up some people to see me get my comeuppance for daring to come back but I didn't pay them much heed. I was interested only in keeping my part of the bargain and behaving as I expect every professional player to behave.

Many were the theories put forward about my failure to live up to expectations, one of them being that I was washed up and over the hill. As soon as a player in any sport creeps over 30 they start writing him off. I was 32 when I ran 60 yards against the quickest defenders in the world to score the most important try of my life. According to some, I'd been slowing up for at least a year before that.

There were several factors which contributed to making the first six months of my union comeback such a disappointment. Not in any particular order, they were: injury, Karen's illness, being played out of position, receiving little support from coaches, being regularly denied good ball on the pitch, the strangeness of the game I'd returned to, lack of big-game motivation and a deterioration of self-confidence and form due to a combination of all these.

The two operations I needed came at the most unfortunate times, and who could fail to be affected while his wife is fighting off a serious illness? But as for influencing the way I played, I believe it is unfair to say that her problems were the cause of mine. One of her main concerns has been that life should be as normal as possible for all the family. She has always been a great supporter of mine throughout my career. She attends most matches and takes more than a wifely interest in how I am playing. It did her morale no favours to see me struggle and for people to think it was because of her illness.

It was the same for me. Any husband whose wife is ill knows the feeling of frustration that there is so little you can do to help. If you could help by strangling a dozen lions then you would happily try. All I could do was to go out and play good rugby to show her that her old man was still capable of providing for our future.

Whenever we've had problems off the field, what I've done on the rugby pitch has helped to solve them. Not this time. We were both fighting battles and she was doing a lot better in hers than I was in mine. I suppose it all added to the strain, but it would still be wrong to say that her problem was making mine worse.

Indeed, it would have helped me more than her if I could have forgotten everything when I was on the pitch. Playing rugby league tends to wipe everything else out of your mind. Unfortunately, union is so slow in comparison and there are so many periods of inactivity that there is no way you can keep outside thoughts from flooding in. Maybe that was part of the trouble: my inability to change down gears to match the slower pace of union.

When Wigan played Bath in May 1996 it was more than a historic encounter, it proved how very much faster and more intensely physical league was. Just as it was understandably difficult for the Bath players to get accustomed to the higher tempo, I think it is almost as difficult to get accustomed to a game that doesn't flow anything like as quickly and continuously. A league game carries you along with it and you have to be sharp and fully concentrated to do well in it. Union, or the Heineken League version of it, was so slow and stop-start that I found it boring, very difficult to concentrate on and hard to get into.

Since Cardiff played such a deliberate and forward-dominated game, it was a harder side than most in which to find my bearings. It would have helped if I could have played in my natural position more often. And this is where the first crunch came.

Even the staunchest critics of my earlier years in union would have to admit that I was an outside half, pure and simple. I played it from the age of nine and everything I achieved in the game was with a No. 10 on my back. More than that, I was an outside half who needed to control things, to be the central pivot of the team. Love me or hate me, that's what I am. I did play the odd game at full-back and, at a pinch, it is the other position I could play in union. What I wasn't, and never will be, was a centre or a wing.

People might have been confused by the fact that I played a lot of my rugby league at centre. In fact, I played every one of the seven positions behind the scrum and I never did settle in any of them. I did play centre a lot, but in league it is a vastly different role. You are one on one with your opposite number and the position does offer many creative options. A union centre, on the other hand, has a more specific responsibility and opponents come at you from all directions. There are too many people on the field in union and you tend to meet a lot of them when you are playing centre.

You didn't have to be a rugby expert to realize that unless my talents were utilized in the way they had been before I left, there wasn't much point in my being there. I quickly got the impression that many of the team agreed and did their best to forget that I was. I got along fine with them socially. I enjoyed their company and found them a super set of lads. But on the pitch I never got rid of the feeling that I was surplus to requirements.

I would have welcomed more support from Terry Holmes, who'd been a hero, friend and inspiration in our past. After Alex's departure, Terry was given the coaching job until the end of the season and obviously his future depended on results. But I suspected there was a clique in the team who stuck closely together and who had an influence in team affairs. I don't blame Terry for placing his faith in the tried and trusted, but in doing so he spoilt any chances I had of fitting in. Maybe he thought that to change the team philosophy to accommodate me might have unbalanced the team and put their prospects at risk. Perhaps he was right. But since they fell short of winning anything he wouldn't have lost out by doing so. I would hate anyone to think that we are not still the best of friends. We just had different opinions at the time.

What concerned me more than anything was a matter I touched on earlier. Many people thought that I was deliberately being denied the ball. Passes that should have come my way went to someone else too often for it not to be noticed. I thought it was odd but shrugged it off. Others didn't. At first, it was just relatives and friends who got indignant about it. Then the press picked it up. Voices would shout from the crowd. Then, strangers would come and ask: 'Why won't Adrian pass to you?' These weren't isolated incidents, they were happening all the time, and they didn't only cite Adrian – they talked about other members of the team.

Never once did I suggest that I was aware of what they were talking about. I could agree that I wasn't getting a fair crack of the whip and that I was being played out of position, but to suggest that fellow professionals were deliberately keeping the ball away from me was something I couldn't accept. There was a certain atmosphere between Adrian and me, but that's natural between rivals for the same position. If there had been any truth in it I would have been bitterly disappointed. It is not something I've ever encountered before. I was aware I wasn't getting much ball, but I couldn't accept that it was planned that way.

It was ironic that when they were trying to get me to be an inside centre I said that Adrian was better suited to that position than me. If I'd played outside half and he at inside centre, we'd have been a much stronger partnership with a pile of options. The idea was rejected. Near the end of the season, when Adrian was in the Welsh training squad and bidding for a place on the Australian tour, he told me after training one night that he didn't think he would make it at outside half but he might have gone as inside centre if he'd played in that position a few times. I couldn't resist the temptation to say I told you so. Had we taken those roles I reckon we'd have won the Cup and league. But who knows?

What I did know was that Cardiff were going to get nowhere with the type of rugby they were playing. As I mentioned before, they were persisting with a mauling game that had made them into a strong side but which was now so predictable that teams could counter it. The fast rucking game that Neath and Pontypridd were playing was the modern tactic. It fitted in with what Wales were trying to do and would bring results.

I'm not blaming anyone at Cardiff, or Alex Evans. Wales hadn't been rucking properly for years. The back-rows had taken control. They all wanted to be ball-carriers and therefore bogged the game down in mauls or rucks from which the ball came out too slowly.

This is the main reason we haven't been producing good outside halves. Welsh teams haven't rucked properly for years. Without fast rucking you don't allow an outside half enough time to be properly creative. One of the few teams who have rucked fast and efficiently over the years has been Neath. It is no accident that I came through with Neath. They were and still are an outside half's dream team. Every creative stand-off in recent times in Wales has been produced by Neath. Arwel Thomas, Adrian Davies, Matthew McCarthy . . . no other team has produced halves of that quality. The tragedy is that they have gone elsewhere and not been as creative because they haven't had the same service. The back-rows have got to return to being fast ruckers and ball-winners. And when they win the ball, they must give it out quickly and let the outside half dictate the game in the best interests of the team. The No. 10 is the eyes of the team.

Back in Llanelli's glory days, Phil Bennett was helped in his brilliance because among his options was a pass to Ray Gravell, who could plough through – and if he couldn't link he would set up another ruck and Phil would get the ball again. This meant that Phil was in full control and he had the ability to make the most of it. These days, even Phil would find the service difficult to work with. The Scots are no better at rugby than Wales, but they've always had a good rucking game. That's why they can produce an outside half like Gregor Townsend.

It doesn't help our rucking game that the referees are so hard on attempts to get rid of players who are lying offside at rucks, stopping the attacking side getting at the ball. In New Zealand the attitude is that the bastard shouldn't be there and deserves a bloody good kicking so he will think twice about doing it again. But here, the players doing the rucking are very often penalized for stamping. I don't hold with stamping – it is a dangerous offence – but very often the referees don't make the distinction.

If a player is lying offside, he is stopping the other team getting quick ball. He is slowing the game down and depriving the spectators of real action. He deserves to be rucked out of the way. A good shoeing is the answer if he is spoiling the game. The referees could be much more vigilant about this.

When Cardiff played Llanelli in the Cup, Gwyn Jones and Mark Perego were offside most of the game. Because we didn't ruck them properly we allowed them to get away with it. Had we rucked them properly, the referee would have had to penalize them or us. We would have forced him to decide.

Whenever one of them lay down on the wrong side of the ball I was yelling, 'Get the shoes into him.' The referee shouted at me, 'Hey, hey, you shouldn't say that.'

But why not? It should have made him aware of what was going on. In my previous rugby union career, I was painfully aware that if I tackled someone and ended up the wrong side of the ball the sight of the No. 10 on my back would bring them pouring in to ruck me to death. I couldn't get out of the way quick enough. Players aren't forced to do that these days, because referees are not doing their job.

At Cardiff I went banging on to anyone who cared to listen about rucking and how we were playing the wrong type of game. After the Llanelli game it appears the message got through. The next game, against Abertillery, we started to play a bit more as I suggested. The only trouble was that I got dropped – relegated to the replacements bench.

We were playing my game and I wasn't in it. I was never to occupy the outside-half position again that season. I played centre twice and scored my first Heineken League try at Treorchy – and my last. It also marked the only really decent pass I'd had in months.

Terry went public with the opinion that Adrian was his first choice. This was even after Adrian announced he was going to play for Richmond the following season. They preferred a player who was leaving to one who was staying.

I asked Terry: 'Do you think he is a better outside half than me?'

'No, but he is better for the team,' he answered. Adrian is a very pleasant and very confident individual and was influential at

Cardiff. Outside Cardiff, however, he had fewer admirers and should have made more of the chances he had at international level. He is the type of player who would help win you the games you ought to win. I prefer the outside half who gets you the unexpected wins.

For the remainder of my return to union, I took my seat on the bench and wondered what the future held for an old-fashioned outside half anxious to revive a few memories.

CHAPTER 7

Small Beginnings

No less an expert than Carwyn James, the legendary Llanelli and British Lions coach, earmarked Jonathan for stardom when the player was only nine years old and under-sized even for that tender age. Two years later he told the youngster, who had barely grown in the interim, that he would play for Wales.

James, a prophet whose country disgracefully failed to honour him with the job of national coach, died at an early age, alas – much too early to see Jonathan get anywhere near the glory he had predicted. Indeed, had the great man seen him as a 16- or 17-year-old he would have despaired at the boy's chances of fulfilling that destiny. It is one thing for a kid's raw potential to be recognized, but quite another for it to be nurtured and guided along the treacherous path to fruition.

The schools are an obvious breeding ground – it was under the beneficial coaching of headmaster Meirion Davies at Trimsaran Primary that Jonathan's talent first prospered – but they aren't always the safe conduit to greater things. Owing to an unfortunate dispute, his schooldays didn't turn out to be his happiest ones.

Neither did the fact that he came from the very heart of Wales's famous outside-half factory appear to be of massive assistance. A ten-mile-square area of land running west from Llanelli to Carmarthen has been responsible for producing a flurry of renowned outside halves including Carwyn himself, Barry John, Phil Bennett, Gareth Davies and Gary Pearce. It is an amazing record, and you would have thought that talent scouts from the major clubs would have had this sacred patch policed day and night for signs of the next emerging star.

But Jonathan managed to avoid close attention until it was almost too late. Carwyn didn't miss him, though. He had been asked to present the prizes in an Under-11 seven-a-side event and select the best player. Jonathan was two years younger and far smaller than most of the players on view, but he was so outstanding that Carwyn had no hesitation in choosing him as player of the tournament. Indeed, he asked the organizers if Jonathan could keep the trophy instead of handing it back the following year. They agreed, and Carwyn bought one to replace it.

They met again two years later. Carwyn, who had seen the youngster play once or twice since and was pleased with his progress, was writing a book which included a chapter on international outside halves of the future. He was certain Jonathan was going to play for Wales and would follow into the team a player whose name Jonathan can't remember and Gareth Davies, who was a little older again.

Jonathan actually took Gareth Davies's place in the Welsh team. The player in between never made it, but to have two out of three right was typical of Carwyn's foresight. Had he survived long enough, it would have been unthinkable that Jonathan would have had to wait until he was 19 before his adult potential was recognized.

But, then, Carwyn saw only a genuinely gifted prospect. Most saw a skinny little boy who was obviously far too small for the hurly-burly of rugby.

Thankfully, there were others who agreed with Ken Williams, who was later to become Jonathan's stepfather. 'He was all nose and hair – there was not much else you could see,' Ken recalls. 'But when he got the ball you'd forget about his size.'

Jonathan was fortunate that his time at Trimsaran Primary School coincided with that of Meirion Davies, who had been born on the outskirts of the village and had returned after spells in London and Cardiff. One of many Welsh teachers who sought their first jobs in London, Meirion played for London Welsh when they were becoming Britain's leading club. He moved back to Wales to teach in Cardiff and played four seasons for the Arms Park club.

The chance of playing for Llanelli brought him back to teach at Trimsaran. As a friend of Jonathan's father, Len, Meirion obviously knew of Jonathan but it wasn't until he set about *organizing a school rugby team that he realized what exceptional potential he had.*

Had Meirion not been a first-class player himself and had the creation of a school team not been a pleasure for him but a chore, Jonathan's development might easily have been stunted before it started. Anyone less sensitive to the various abilities necessary to be a success at rugby would have been likely, with the very best of intentions, to divert him to less arduous sporting pursuits.

But Meirion saw more than just a puny frame. 'Although he was very, very small he was outstanding from the very beginning. It was sheer talent with the ball that marked him out – and that was with any type of ball. All the good outside halves in Welsh rugby would have made excellent soccer players, Barry John and Phil Bennett especially, and Jonathan would have been the same. But he was totally committed to rugby. I don't remember seeing him without a rugby ball under his arm and he mastered the skills at a very early age.'

Meirion was determined that his boys would learn rugby as a handling game. 'I encouraged them to run and pass the ball as much as possible. Kicking was an option when all else had failed. Jonathan responded magnificently. He was two years younger than most of those around him and yet his was the mature mind, always willing to try things.'

Jonathan's size was something the boy himself would often bring up as a disadvantage. Meirion would reason with him that many schoolboy rugby players excelled because they were bigger and stronger than their contemporaries. Once they grew up and the size difference was eliminated so was their superiority. Jonathan was a good player without the size, he still had that to come.

'But he didn't develop physically until quite late. He must have been 17 or 18 before he began to grow substantially. He is not big now but he was late even getting to that stage. There was no doubt his size held him back; not in development but in people's acceptance of him. This was unfair because he was always a keen tackler, very anxious to do his bit for the team. He wasn't able to meet them head-on all the time, but he would get them down one way or another. It was never a problem with him. It was *as if he had to prove that his size was not a handicap, and neither was it. He did more tackling than any outside half of recent memory, other than David Watkins.'*

Meirion Davies did something else for Jonathan. He used the boy's love for rugby to help him scholastically. When the 11-plus exam neared, Meirion put his foot down. No studying, no rugby. If the homework wasn't up to scratch the miscreant wouldn't be in the team. Jonathan didn't miss a match – and passed.

But winning a place at Gwendraeth Grammar School was a mixed blessing. It was a fine school with a great tradition for producing rugby stars, but it took Jonathan away from his friends and into a world where he would have to prove all over again that his size was not a problem.

It had been a recurring theme of his life that he has repeatedly found himself faced with new situations and problems which he doubts he can overcome.

Now that rugby union is professional, I trust that we will see a far more thorough and satisfying way of recruiting youngsters to the game and ensuring they get every opportunity to realize their potential. Too many have been lost to rugby because they didn't come from the right place or go to the right school.

Good players have suddenly become so valuable that even England can't ignore the vast numbers of youngsters who do not get proper exposure to rugby because of their background.

I was amazingly lucky that before reaching the age of ten I came under the influence of three men who were not only very good players but wise with it. The first was my father Len, the second was my primary school teacher Meirion Davies, and the third was the great Carwyn James. My dealings with Carwyn were very brief, but he was a god where I came from, and the few words of encouragement he gave me were worth a fortune to the puniest boy around.

The three of them gave me what no one else could have – the confidence to disregard my size as a handicap and allow my natural instincts to rule my game. Without their presence at that stage of my life, there was no way I would have become a rugby player. I was so ill-equipped for the game physically that I would have eventually given in to all the dissuasion I used to receive.

My father was no giant himself. He was bigger than I am but neither tall nor sturdy for a centre. He had this speed, though, and with the ball in his hands was very elusive. According to some shrewd judges I was never as quick or as nimble as him. He played for Swansea, then for Llanelli, and finished his career as captain of Trimsaran. He was playing for Swansea when he married my mother in 1960, and they lived at first in his home village of Llwynhendy, which is on the Swansea side of Llanelli and near to the Trostre steelworks, where he worked in the buying department.

Oddly enough, my father had an offer to go north before they were married. She was 18 and he was 25. It was a tempting offer: £2,000 to join Leigh. He turned it down, because he had the responsibility of looking after his grandmother, but his fellow centre, Gordon Lewis, had a similar offer and accepted. Gordon went on to make 379 appearances for Leigh. Although he thought my father was a very good player he wasn't sure how he would have coped in league. Gordon was altogether bigger, and yet he ended up in hospital twice in his first three games.

Had my father gone I would have been born there and most likely would have been a league player from the outset. Although my size would have been a problem there, too, they are more inclined to see what you are made of before they dismiss you.

I'll happily settle for the upbringing I had in Trimsaran. My mother and father moved there two years later, when I was due, to share the home of my mother's parents. Trimsaran is a mining village five miles over the mountain from Llanelli and on the western edge of a coalfield that produced the finest anthracite in the world. The place was the cradle of my life and my career.

My father never weighed me down with the expectation that I was to follow him as a first-class rugby player, but succeeded in giving me two vital attributes – the love of a ball and a hatred of losing.

When I had reached the toddling stage, he was seeing out his career with a good Trimsaran side and he had plenty of time to play with me. I can't remember him bombarding me with advice but he did bombard me with the ball, any ball. Soccer ball, cricket ball, tennis ball . . . we played with them all for hours.

He put me under no pressure to favour a rugby ball, but whenever Trimsaran were playing I was a ballboy and when I wasn't chasing to retrieve the match-ball I had my own to kick, catch and throw. Gradually, the ball became an extension of me and I felt completely at home with it. The relationship is still strong. I'm not always sure which way it is going to bounce when I'm chasing it, but I'll bet my guess against anyone else's.

This feel for the ball was my father's greatest gift to me, and I'm trying to pass on the same heirloom to my son Scott. Cluttering the minds of children with theory can be harmful to the development of natural ability, and parents who stand on the touchline yelling advice can do a lot of damage. My father believed in the value of coaching, but first of all he believed in letting the ball work its own magic.

The next thing to be learned, for which I needed no teacher, was that the world was full of bigger people who wanted to take your precious ball off you.

At my first press conference after joining Widnes, I was asked where my speed came from.

'Fear,' I answered.

They all roared with laughter and wrote about how witty I was. But I wasn't joking. I'd never been a particularly fast runner at school. I was always second to a boy named David Jenkins in the cross-country, and although I was always there or thereabouts in the sprints I was no faster than many of my friends.

We always used to have family running races on the beach at Tenby, and I was 14 years old before I could beat my mother; so I did not grow up with any great faith in my pace. But when I had the ball in my hands on a rugby pitch I seemed to be able to run like the wind. Fear could have been the only cause of that. I was invariably the smallest on the pitch and the incentive to avoid being caught was considerable.

I was five or six when I first realized the advantages of being a slippery customer. In front of the houses on the council estate we lived in was a small strip of lawn that served its purpose as a pitch for a game of three-a-side that would rarely end until my side had won. That was the other gift my father gave me: the will to win. I doubt if mine has ever matched his. Few people like losing, but with him it was a passionate hatred. This was displayed not only on the rugby field, where one or two notable last-minute victories were achieved because of his refusal to accept defeat, but also everywhere. If he lost a friendly game of darts he thought he should have won, he was prone to go straight home leaving his unfinished pint on the bar.

He never once let me win anything. Draughts, snap, snakes and ladders, blow-football . . . he did me no favours. He played to beat me, and instilled in me a competitive spirit I wouldn't be without, although it did get the better of me once or twice in my younger days.

I once threw a tantrum after an adult team from Llandovery beat Trimsaran Youth in a sevens tournament. I was so upset I kicked the ball high into a tree. The referee, who happened to be Clive Norling, made me climb up and fetch it. I learned the lesson – I'm still a bad loser but I try hard not to show it.

When we finally outgrew the patch of grass in front of the house we had to move to the recreation ground, where our self-organized mayhem continued, not only in rugby but in soccer and cricket. Even in school we ran our own games because Trimsaran Primary didn't have any organized sports teams. But that all changed, and probably my life with it, when Meirion Davies arrived as a teacher and immediately set about creating a rugby team to compete with other schools in the area.

Heaven had suddenly arrived. Here was a man who had played for a few of the best teams in Britain and he was anxious to supervise our indisciplined efforts. But he didn't impose himself. All he did was to harness what raw talent he saw, and in no time his influence was bearing fruit. As a seven-a-side team we quickly became the undisputed champions of the area.

Since I was less than nine years old he had to ask permission from my parents – he was a friend of my father, so he was confident of the answer – to play me in the full school side in the Under-11 league. Nigel Davies, Andrew John and Carl Bridge-water were among those who benefited so much from Meirion's arrival and went on to enjoy careers in first-class rugby. It was a time of sheer bliss. He moulded us into the best team around without affecting our natural abilities.

Small as I was, he made the best use of my speed and my love of handling the ball. He discouraged kicking as an easy option and encouraged me in my sense of adventure and my willingness to try the unexpected. It is vital that rugby union attempts to make sure that as many youngsters as possible have the sort of experience that did so much for us in Trimsaran. Without the foundation Meirion provided, none of us might have made it.

One major bonus of what we achieved at Trimsaran Primary was that, at the age of 11, I was selected to play for West Wales against East Wales at the National Stadium in Cardiff in an Under-12s curtain-raiser to the Wales v. Tonga international in 1974. So my father did at least see me wear a red shirt at the Arms Park. That was the last opportunity he had, and whether he saw a future international in me that day is hard to say. He and my mother had seats right at the back of the new north stand, from where, my mother recalls, I looked like a red ant.

While Meirion continued to give me valuable advice for years afterwards, my schooldays at Trimsaran came to a sad end. Thanks to Meirion's teaching I passed my 11-plus but I was not pleased at the result. It meant that I was to attend Gwendraeth Grammar School. This pleased my father, because he had qualified to go there but wasn't able to undertake the long daily journey because he had to look after his grandmother. It also happened to be the best school a budding outside half could possibly attend. Carwyn James went there, as did Barry John and Gareth Davies – a fly-half factory if ever there was one.

But I didn't want to go there. I had set my heart on Stradey Comprehensive, which was close to Stradey Park, home of my beloved Llanelli RFC. My mother had gone there, and most of my rugby-playing friends were going there because they'd failed the exam.

My first day at Gwendraeth was absolute misery. Karen Hopkins from Cefneithin, who was to become my wife, was another new pupil that day but I was much less interested in sharing a classroom with girls than I was in being robbed of my friends.

It probably went a lot deeper than that. Being small and skinny is no great advantage in any situation, apart from the Indian rope trick, but at least in Trimsaran my rugby ability had given me some social muscle. I was somebody. But at Gwendraeth I was merely small and skinny and a long way off qualifying to play for one of the school teams. My parents tried their best to cheer me up. My father had started to run a youth team for Trimsaran RFC and he used to say that it wouldn't be long before I was playing for them. By the time I did, he had passed away.

In the first couple of years at Gwendraeth, my rugby did not advance very far. The school teams were of an age level that put them just out of my reach and I had to convince people all over again that my size was no reflection on my ability. But even when I got into the team, it was tough going. Despite its reputation for producing sports stars, the school had only 600 pupils and was heavily outnumbered by the giant comprehensives and larger grammar schools. As a result, we were continually meeting bigger and better teams.

It was not easy to shine when the team was seeing little of the ball and getting a battering in the process. I managed to get picked for the district, but the same problem applied. Our district was Mynydd Mawr, which did not have a big catchment area, so when we played Cardiff district, or Swansea or Bridgend, the difference in size between the packs meant a slim ration of the ball for the backs.

There was something else difficult to live with, the ghosts of Gwendraeth's past. People would look at me struggling to make the most of meagre ball and say: 'He's no Barry John' or 'He'll never make a Gareth Davies.'

It was at this time, too, that the world was starting to cave in at home. We were living next door to my grandparents, to whom I was very close. My grandfather was forever lecturing me on the amount of time I spent at rugby instead of my homework, but I was still extremely fond of him. One night he was knocked down by a motor-car and, typically of him, he apologized to the driver. He eventually died of his injuries.

I was 12 years of age, and when my dog Ben died soon afterwards it convinced me that the world had become an unpleasant place. Life, however, was merely preparing me for the calamity that was to come.

The fateful signs were not long in appearing. At first my father seemed to be suffering from an attack of yellow jaundice, but his condition worsened and doctors at Llanelli hospital diagnosed liver cancer. His only hope was a transfer to the famous Addenbrooke's Hospital, Cambridge, where they were beginning to attempt liver transplants. They were more advanced in Cape Town and San Francisco, but he couldn't afford to go there.

It was an appalling time for my mother, who made no attempt to hide the seriousness of the situation from me although my younger sister Caroline was kept in the dark. My mother came to look very ill herself. Not only was the prospect harrowing, but the journey from Trimsaran to Cambridge by public transport could hardly have been more difficult.

Once there she stayed in a bed-sitter, spending as much time as permitted at the hospital. We couldn't have asked for a more brilliant surgeon than Professor Roy Calne, but he left us in no doubt about the risks. Dad was to be the first Welshman to receive a liver transplant, and only the third Briton.

My mother took me up with her just before the operation, and when I left his bedside to wait outside for her, I thought I would never see him again. I went into the hospital chapel and prayed. I'd pretended to pray many times in Sunday school. Now, at just turned 13, I was praying hard for the first time in my life.

Professor Calne's operation was a great success. My father became a celebrity patient. He was even introduced to Princess Margaret as one of their successes when she visited the Addenbrooke's liver unit.

He still needed constant treatment, requiring two visits to Carmarthen and one to Cambridge every week, but at least we had him back. We even made it to the beach at Tenby that summer where we played bowls together with that same competitive edge.

But it was too good to last. Although the transplant continued to be a success, the cancer was present in other parts of his body. It was back to Cambridge where he had more severe surgery. He wanted to know all about my rugby when my mother took me with her, but it was clear he was fighting a losing battle.

One day the deputy headmaster came into the classroom and asked for me. I had been playing football during the break and I hit Alun Griffiths in the ear with the ball. He was crying and said he'd gone deaf. So, at first, I thought I was being called out to be punished. Then it dawned on me. Before the teacher said anything, I said: 'My father's dead isn't he?'

The village had been a great help through his long illness. The rugby club held a Past v. Present game to raise funds for my mother's fares to Cambridge. After his funeral, which was a week before Christmas, a neighbour asked my mother what plans she had made. She said we wouldn't be bothering. They weren't going to allow that, and she was marched down to the shops and assisted to buy a couple of presents for me and Caroline and the basic festive things.

My mother had behaved brilliantly under the strain of that year or so. She lost so much weight and nothing seemed to go right as she tried to restore the family to an even keel. She took a job in the school canteen to help our finances, but had a problem she was desperate to solve. When Dad was alive, we used to go everywhere in our car, a navy-blue Morris 1000 whose number plate, TTH 372D, I will never forget. But Mammy couldn't drive and, apart from the practical advantages in having a car in an out-of-the-way place, Caroline and I missed our little outings.

Although she hardly needed the hassle, she took up driving lessons. However, twice she took the test and twice she had to come home and tell us that she'd failed. I don't think we were as sympathetic as we should have been. She passed at the third attempt and life returned to a more convenient state.

When my mother eventually remarried, we were very fortunate in her choice. Ken Williams, a Trimsaran man born and bred, played in the village team with my father and had experienced his own tragedy. His wife Phyllis, one of my mother's closest friends, died at the age of 29 from leukaemia, leaving him with a son, Peter, who is a few years older than me.

The joining of the two families strengthened everyone concerned and was of particular benefit to me. Ken brought the close support of a father, at a crucial time, and that's how I think of him now. I will miss my father for the rest of my life and bitterly regret he hasn't been able to share in the success he wanted for me. But I don't feel deprived because my mother and Ken, another rugby man through and through, have done so much to compensate.

It was a few years, however, before I showed any sign of success at rugby and there followed an unfortunate incident that turned my life upside down.

I was 17 and the not-so-proud possessor of two O-levels. Nevertheless, I was proceeding with my A-levels in the faint hope that I might win a Welsh schools cap. I hadn't been anywhere near it beforehand but things were going a little better. As well as being in the school team, I was playing for Trimsaran Youth when school fixtures allowed, and I had won my way into the East Dyfed Under-17 county team as well.

Then came the most exciting letter I had ever received. It was from the Welsh Schools Rugby Union (Senior Group) inviting me to attend the week's course for potential international players at Aberystwyth that summer. It was the customary get-together of players they considered likely to be challenging for places in the Welsh senior schoolboys' team the following season.

It was April 1980, I was seventeen and a half years old, still small but starting to fill out, and somebody had fed me a dream. I had time to reflect on it because I was ill and off school when the letter arrived. My head must have been in the clouds when I received a garbled message via a friend that I had been picked to play for East Dyfed against Mid Glamorgan in the semi-final of the Welsh county competition. There was no official notification and at the time I wasn't even sure I'd be fit to play.

Then came an SOS from Trimsaran Youth. They were playing in the Llanelli & District Cup Final and because of injuries had only 14 players. Could I play?

Needless to say, the Trimsaran final was on the same evening as the East Dyfed match. I felt well enough to play, but who for? My mother and I talked about it for hours.

There was no doubt who I wanted to play for. Many of my boyhood pals were playing for Trimsaran Youth, and it was the team my father founded with Ray James and Haydn Ford. It was Trimsaran who raised money to help my mother visit my father in Cambridge. I hadn't heard officially I was wanted by East Dyfed. As far as they knew I was ill.

In the end, there seemed no way I could turn down Trimsaran. It would have been some consolation had we won, but we didn't.

Two days later my mother received a letter from Alan Lewis, the PE master at Gwendraeth. It read:

'I was extremely disappointed to learn that Jonathan had played on Tuesday for Trimsaran Youth. He had previously been selected to represent East Dyfed on the same evening and obviously the first loyalty of all pupils is to school rugby. Furthermore, had the proper procedure been adhered to, Trimsaran RFC should have sought my written permission to play any Gwendraeth Grammar School boy.

'Consequently, I have contacted Mr E.J. Williams, WSSRU coach, concerning the matter and it has been decided that Jonathan will not now be able to attend the selected course at Aberystwyth and another outside half will be found to take his place.'

The following day I received a letter from Mr Williams which spoke of his 'extreme disappointment' and 'a serious breach of the rules' and confirmed that I had been withdrawn from the course.

Even in a house so familiar with bad times, the dejection was deep. But my mother was determined not to let it rest there. She wrote back to Williams seeking to put one or two things right, particularly the allegation that I had been disloyal to the school:

'Jonathan has played rugby for Gwendraeth for the last five and a half years, two of those years being very difficult for us all because my husband died leaving us a little hard up. Jonathan was offered a weekend job which would have brought in about £15– £20, but we had a little conference and decided that he should be free to play rugby for the school on Saturday. Many boys from the village and Gwendraeth did take jobs but we thought his first concern should be to the school. I now realize it was a very wrong decision.

'I hope this letter will help your committee to see that Jonathan is not a disloyal boy and that his only weakness is that his heart is too big and he tries to please everyone. I hope that if he does manage to go further in his rugby career that this one mistake will not be held against him.'

Her plea brought no response and it was not long before my mother was writing again. This time it was in defence of Trimsaran RFC, who had been reported to the Welsh Rugby Union over the incident. She told them the full story; that I had been ill and away from school; that I had been informed of the East Dyfed game unofficially and even then by a garbled word of mouth message; that she had contributed to my decision by reminding me that we owed a debt of gratitude to the club. She offered to attend the hearing personally.

Once more, her words fell on deaf ears. Trimsaran Youth were banned from playing rugby for the first month of the following season.

I was more annoyed for my mother's sake than for mine, because she had worked so hard to reduce the effect of losing a father on me and Caroline, and she took it so hard that she had been unable to prevent this setback to my rugby career. I certainly didn't blame her, but the incident didn't help to convince me that fate was working in my favour.

Two years or so later, Alan Lewis called at the house. As well as being PE master at Gwendraeth he was now the coach of Pontadulais, who play in the West Wales League. He was hoping I would sign for them. I was out at the time and Ken sent him away with a flea in his ear.

But Alan and I became good friends later, which is just as well. At about the same time I joined the WRU as development officer in November 1995, Alan joined the Union as assistant coach to Kevin Bowring!

I think we both regret what happened and it certainly got out of all proportion. I still can't believe how savage the punishment was for my offence. To effectively bar me from playing for Welsh schools for an entire season, which meant for ever, was a sentence I would have expected if I'd burned the school down.

My dreams having been destroyed, there didn't seem any point in continuing at school. My relationship with Alan was obviously strained and my prospects of school rugby of any sort looked a bit grim. My A-level studies were not so gripping that I couldn't bear to abandon them, so I decided that since Trimsaran offered the only decent chance of a game of rugby I would step into the outside world.

I didn't regard it as a calamity, especially as my relationship with Karen was coming to a halt. Since she was one of the few reasons why school was bearable, the place had no further hold on me.

Unfortunately, there was not a wide choice of career opportunities available, and the family came to the quick and unanimous decision that I should follow my stepbrother Peter into the painting and decorating trade. So I signed up for a three-year apprenticeship.

CHAPTER 8

Neath to the Rescue

Jonathan was once offered a place at Cambridge University. It wasn't when he was a struggling teenager, painting council houses for a living and dodging the lunging tackles that can make the West Wales league an uncomfortable place for a wisp of a boy; it was years later when he was already established as the brightest outside half of his generation.

Cambridge would have been happy to provide a sports scholarship in return for his services in a light-blue jersey. However, even at the height of his fame, Jonathan still needed to earn a living and was obliged to forgo the experience, much as he relished the idea of marching into the hallowed seat of learning armed with two O-levels, one for Welsh and the other for geography.

But he did go to the Varsity match the following December. He was invited to speak at a pre-match luncheon in one of the swish marquees they erect at Twickenham for the occasion. There, at the very heart of English amateurism, he was slipped an envelope containing £400 in notes.

(He was invited back to perform the same function the following year, by which time he had become a rugby league player. They gave him a cheque for £250. When he questioned the discrepancy they explained that professionals didn't command as high a fee because no rules were being broken. Amateurs were more expensive.)

But all that was in a future the like of which seemed hardly possible when Jonathan left his A-levels unfinished and began painting his first drainpipe. It was to be another two years before he would get his chance in first-class rugby. Before that came he would suffer a demoralizing rejection by Llanelli and, after it, a serious injury that took months out of a career barely started.

In some ways, his early misfortunes gave him the resilience to absorb these blows. His mother had noticed this early maturing with alarm at first. Because he was small he used his aggression and skill at sport to win respect, and these qualities brought him the company, friendship and protection of bigger boys. He was inclined to lead rather than follow, and at one time Diana was concerned that he was turning into a bit of a bully, a small-time gang boss.

The phase passed quickly but he still had a magnetic personality and was full of the hospitality that had been bred into him. He was rarely without a group of friends. He would bring three or four home for lunch, tea or a late-night movie on television, and the household often rose in the morning to find several boys sleeping in the softer places around the house.

Quite how mature he was did not dawn on his mother until her husband died. When Jonathan came home early from school that day, she expected that a distraught 14-year-old would be another burden to bear, but it was she who found consolation in his calmness and control.

'He was wonderful,' Diana recalls. 'Not only was he able to cope with his own feelings, he tried to help me cope with mine. Without being asked, it was Jonathan who took visitors into the front room to pay their last respects to Len. He saw it as his duty and I was proud of the way he did it.

'Christmas was a week later and I was dreading it. But he read that situation, too, and kept up a non-stop barrage of silly jokes that brought laughter to a home that badly needed it.'

If Neath hadn't been so desperate for an outside half, I might never have had the chance to play first-class rugby. As an opportunity it could hardly be described as golden, but I was over 19 years of age when they called me up and time was running out so quickly that even a fleeting chance looked inviting to me.

To put it into perspective, I was to be the 13th outside half Neath had tried that season. The phrase 'scraping the barrel' comes to mind. As a matter of fact, the day they contacted me I had been watching a televised recording of their game against Bridgend the previous afternoon in which they were hammered. Karen remembers me saying how awful it must be to play for a team like that.

A couple of hours later, they rang to offer to share the experience with me. I was playing for Trimsaran at the time and it was normal for bigger clubs to take players on permit for one match so that they could have a close look at them. I'd had offers from larger clubs in the West Wales league but I'd always turned them down. Neath were different. They were struggling but they were one of the great clubs, and the chance to play for them against Pontypridd on the following Tuesday night could not be resisted. I wasn't flattered that they'd tried 12 others before they got around to me, but neither was I in a position to be haughty about it.

My hopes had been at ground level since the previous summer, when I had been turned down out of hand after a trial with my beloved Llanelli. I was distraught because I had allowed my optimism to run wild.

After the Gwendraeth incident, I left school and quickly slipped comfortably into a life of work and rugby that was very enjoyable. I happily sloshed paint around and spent most spare moments playing rugby with my pals in Trimsaran Youth. I still had my ambitions. I still wanted to play first-class rugby, preferably for Llanelli and for Wales, and although the rest of the world was being a bit slow in fitting in with my dreams I don't remember any impatience.

And I could play for Trimsaran without breaking any rules. There was the small matter of the month's ban my Gwendraeth episode had incurred, but that merely meant that most of us played in Trimsaran's second team in the first month of the following season.

So I found myself involved in adult rugby of a sort that doesn't take kindly to little whippersnappers, particularly cheeky ones. It brought home the reality that I wasn't a schoolboy any more. I was standing shoulder to shoulder with real men, only my shoulder was at least a foot lower than most of theirs.

Once Trimsaran Youth got under way again, we began to have an excellent season, topped by reaching the semi-final of the Welsh Youth Cup. What helped us enormously was that Meirion Davies had by that time become Trimsaran's coach. The principles he drilled into us at a very young age were therefore reinforced at this later stage of our development.

At the end of that season I was 18 and was sufficiently confident to put my name forward for a trial with Llanelli. It was the summer of 1981, and when I was invited to take part in a trial match at Stradey I could feel destiny calling.

I can't remember everything about the game, but I scored a try and finished feeling pretty pleased with myself. After the match I waited for someone to say something. Like most of the young trialists that day, I searched the faces of the Llanelli coaches for some sign of recognition. But they singled out a few, and for the rest of us it was a case of 'don't call us, we'll call you'.

My impression was that they felt I looked a bit feeble. It was not a reaction I was surprised at, but that didn't ease the pain of rejection at the one place where I thought they'd be more interested in ability than size. To have been dismissed after one brief look by the club I idolized, without one word of encouragement or explanation, left me numb with disappointment.

It brought my head down from the clouds and made me realize that I had fallen a long way behind my ambitions. Rugby is such an intense part of life in that area that to have reached the age of 18 without some major recognition of your talent is to be virtually written off in terms of real potential.

My size was the main problem. From the time I was eight, whenever people have seen me for the first time they've had trouble taking me seriously as a rugby player. And they remain sceptical until they've seen me play a few times and I've forced them to change their minds. It happened when I went to Neath, when I played for Wales, when I went to Widnes, when I played for Great Britain, when I went to Australia . . . It probably still happens!

At 18 I was a lot smaller and certainly less robust-looking than I am now, and this need to break down people's prejudice about my size before I could impress them was a big burden. I was convinced that my lack of representative honours at school was due to the fact that one look at me was usually enough for most selectors. This is why being chosen for that course at Aberystwyth was all the more important and why losing my place on it was a bitter blow to my prospects. Had I played for Welsh schools that season, I would have had all the exposure I needed.

It might even have helped me to get a place in university, and who knows what would have happened then. I might have studied for one of the professions, become a fat-cat at Harlequins and lived happily ever after. That's the sort of career path that really got you places in rugby union in those days.

I still regret not studying harder at school, but when you are as crazy about sport as I was it is very easy to be diverted. Had my father lived, I think I would have achieved much more at school. It wasn't that my mother didn't badger me about my work but, with all she had to do, there was a limit to her control over me. I could hear a ball bounce from 100 yards away, and I'd be gone.

I will try hard not to let my children be enticed away from their studies but, somehow, I don't feel deprived. In some way, being cast out into the cruel world with nothing but my hopes was good for me. Playing with adults at an early age at least convinced me that my size was not going to be a handicap. I might have trouble convincing others but it was important that I didn't have a hang-up about it.

My self-belief was difficult to maintain after the Llanelli rejection, but here again I had cause to be grateful to Meirion Davies. He urged me to devote myself whole-heartedly to playing in Trimsaran's first team. A season in the hard West Wales scene would give me experience I wouldn't get anywhere else and provide a chance to show what I was worth.

It helped that Trimsaran were playing my type of rugby: a running game that enabled me to sharpen my handling skills against tough and competitive opponents and allowed me to improvise and create. When I wasn't working, I was training. I worked on my speed and strength and could feel myself improving. I was playing in the sort of rugby where tackling could not be shirked. I've always liked tackling, and that season gave me ample opportunity to work on my techniques.

The Llanelli experience had taught me that talent was not enough. You had to work and sweat to gain the strength and stamina to impose your talent on the game. The same attitude served me well when I joined Widnes. The bigger the challenge, the fitter you have to be.

My reward came unexpectedly. I was at the rugby club watching television one Sunday evening when someone opened the door of the lounge and shouted that I was wanted on the telephone.

'Who is it?' I shouted back, reluctant to take my eyes off the set.

'David Shaw, fixture secretary of Neath,' came the answer.

Every eye in the club watched me dash to the phone. They said I'd gone a funny colour when I came back into the bar.

'They want me to play for Neath against Pontypridd on Tuesday,' I announced.

I found out much later that Neath had been encouraged to give me a try by one of my boyhood heroes, Phil Bennett. Phil was the Llanelli outside half who took over from Barry John in the Welsh team and the British Lions. Although he wasn't born in Trimsaran, his mother lived there and so we claimed him as our own. I used to watch him with wide-eyed admiration when my father took me to watch Llanelli. To get his recommendation was a thrill in itself.

Within a couple of hours, a large proportion of the village had made arrangements to make the 20-mile journey to Neath. A coach was booked, carloads were arranged, and those who were due to work were rapidly trying to swap shifts.

Trimsaran is that sort of place. Ever since my father died it was as if the village had assumed his role in our family, and we never lacked a helping hand. And they took a parental interest in my rugby progress that ensured I had a following from home every time I played.

My stepfather, Ken, was in charge of the family outing. He finished his morning shift as chargehand at the coal disposal plant and prepared the car to take me, my mother, my sister Caroline and Karen, who by then was firmly established as my girlfriend and future fiancée. When we collected her at Cefneithin on the way, she couldn't believe how grey my face was. I impressed her further by trembling uncontrollably all the way to the Gnoll.

The place was deserted. So determined were we not to be late that we turned up almost two hours too early. It was a cold February day and not one for hanging about, but after my wait for a chance it didn't seem a long time. Strangely enough, although I looked as if I might die any moment through nervousness, I felt an inner confidence I had never experienced before.

The first person I saw while I waited around with my neatly ironed kit burning a hole in my holdall was Ken Davies, one of the Neath committee men. He'd never seen me before and wondered who the nervous little boy was. When I introduced myself I could see the familiar look of disbelief as he looked me over. But he was very helpful and kind to me and eventually became a close friend.

At that moment he was more concerned with the plight of Neath RFC, who badly needed a reversal of fortunes. Any resemblance between me and a saviour would have been very scant but he politely led me into the Neath dressing-room where he left me to await the rest of the team. Fortunately for me, the first player to turn up was Elgan Rees, the Welsh international winger and one of their best players.

I hung up my clothes on the peg next to his. I was to keep the same peg for the next four years, although I often felt it was a mistake. Elgan is a real gentleman and was one of the best dressed players in the game. Being young and impressionable, I tried to emulate him. But no matter what I wore, or how much I paid for it, Elgan always made me feel as if I'd been kitted out by Oxfam.

That night, however, the only appearance I was worried about was the one I was about to make, and Elgan talked me through the waiting minutes, keeping me as calm as possible. Knowing what a difference it made to me, I have tried ever since to do the same for young players making their debuts.

What with Elgan's encouragement and the feel of Neath's famous Maltese Cross emblem on the breast of my black shirt, I went out with fewer nerves than I expected. I found the game much quicker than I was used to, but I had the confidence to follow my instincts.

It was a close game and I was delighted to help swing it Neath's way by dribbling over the Pontypridd line and dropping on the ball for a try. Towards the end of the game, I dropped a goal almost from the half-way line to make the final score 19–13. To make my day complete I was chosen Man of the Match by the former Wales and British Lions captain John Dawes.

Dawes had gone before I reached the bar from the dressing-room, but he'd been having a chat with the family. When the conversation got around to outside halves, he said he thought the next Welsh No. 10 would be Paul Turner of Newport. Paul did play for Wales, but not until seven years later in 1989, after I'd gone north.

But I was still a long way from thinking about playing for Wales. I was just happy to have made my mark. Neath wanted me to play more matches under permit, but I was a little wary. My first loyalty was to Trimsaran and I was also in with a good chance of being picked for the Welsh Districts team who were going to West Germany in the summer to play the Army. It was my first chance to represent Wales, and if I played more than five games for Neath I would be ineligible.

Although I did play a few more times for Neath at the end of that season, I concentrated on Trimsaran and we finished in style. We won our league, the Llanelli and District Cup, and reached the quarter-finals of the Welsh Brewers' Cup. Then came the news that I was in the Districts team. I was going to do two things I'd never done before – represent Wales and go abroad.

I have to confess that I faked my fitness for the trip. I'd been troubled by a back injury that gave me a lot of pain, but I was determined not to be robbed of another chance to play for Wales which, for all I knew, could have been my last. I reported as being fit and, thankfully, I was able to make a full contribution to a match that we won. I got away with it, but I've never done that since and the memory still makes me feel uncomfortable.

Everyone in Trimsaran was resigned to the fact that I would be leaving the village team. Neath didn't give me much chance to think about it. Ken Davies was around with the transfer forms as soon as I returned from Germany. He said they were worried that Llanelli or Swansea would snap me up. I neglected to tell him that Llanelli had already turned me down and that Swansea had made only a tentative approach!

So I happily signed, not realizing that my successful career with them was about to be painfully delayed in my first appearance as a fully fledged Neath player.

I had joined in time to play for them in the big Snelling Sevens tournament at the National Stadium in Cardiff that preceded the season. Once more, a convoy of villagers left Trimsaran to support me.

To my delight, Neath were drawn in the same pool as Llanelli. It was exactly a year since my abortive trial with them and I tried hard to make them feel sorry. Although I scored a try the result was a 12–12 draw. We both then had to play Newbridge. We beat them, and Llanelli didn't; so at least I had the satisfaction of seeing them drop out of the tournament.

We went on to meet Abertillery in the quarter-finals and felt confident about our ability to go all the way. We beat Abertillery but I didn't finish the game. Early in the second half I felt my knee ligaments go. It was ridiculously simple, there was no one near me, and yet I knew immediately that something serious had happened.

Had I gone straight to see a surgeon, I would have saved a lot of pain and trouble and I would have saved a year of my playing career. But no one advised me to do that, as they would today.

I just rested it, and it seemed to get better, so everyone was convinced it would mend itself. But every time I tried to play, it would start hurting. So I would rest for another couple of weeks and try again. This went on for ages. Then I played a match against Bedford and attempted to come off my right foot to sidestep an opponent. There was a sickening feeling as it gave way. I still kept running and could hear the wing forward pounding after me. I put a grubber kick through with my good left foot and ran straight off the pitch. I'm not sure if the wing forward followed me but I did it all in one movement. It was pointless waiting to be taken off. I knew my knee was wrecked.

My mother and I decided that we would seek out a surgeon who knew about these things and went to see Mr Maldwyn Griffith of Glangwili Hospital in Carmarthen. We waited four and a half hours and still didn't see him because he had an emergency.

We were luckier next time, although lucky hardly describes being told by an expert how badly torn the ligaments were. He said my only chance was a complicated operation known as the Macintosh Repair. If I didn't have it I would never play rugby again.

Before I could react, my mother asked: 'Where do we sign?'

But arranging the operation and getting it done were two very different matters. Already, months had been wasted before the extent of my injury had been diagnosed. Now there was to be another frustrating delay as my name was added to the bottom of a very long waiting list.

I needed two operations while I played in league, and for both I was whipped into hospital very sharply. The two ops I needed during my first few months at Cardiff were performed even quicker. But between damaging my knee in August 1982 and appearing under the lights over Maldwyn Griffith's operating table a full eight months had gone by.

I am not blaming Maldwyn. In fact, I became very friendly with him and his secretary Nellie. They were friendly and helpful, and brilliant with it. The operation was a great success and I have not had a twinge from that knee since.

But had I been better known or belonged to a more fashionable club, that delay would have been unthinkable. I'd never heard of private medicine, and although attempts were made by the club to speed things up, they were in vain. It was not only my rugby career that was being seriously interrupted: my job was under threat because I couldn't climb a ladder.

When people talk of the good old days of true blue rugby amateurism it is as well to remember that for many players the disadvantages of being a playing servant for rugby's Corinthians were not all connected with the absence of money. Players from a wealthier background, who are playing for the bigger and better clubs, have always enjoyed better medical treatment.

Although the operation had been a success there was still a long and painful road back to the game. Once more, I was fortunate in having Phil Bennett watching over me. Having suffered a similar injury, he advised me on the way to restore my wasted muscles and the tears of pain it would be necessary to shed.

Ken took two rails out of the landing banisters so I could dangle my legs over the stairs. I put a weight on my foot and sat there for hours bending and straightening my knee until I could bear it no more.

When I was able to run, I pounded up and down Trimsaran mountain. I loaded a sock with sand and wrapped it round my ankle to make the running harder. Then someone in the village found an old army bandolier and filled the pouches with iron filings. I looked even more odd on my daily runs.

After five months I was able to resume light training and eventually faced the moment of truth when I tested the knee in a reserve match. I scored a try within 50 seconds and the knee stood up to every pressure I put it under. A few more reserve games, I thought, and I'll be asking for my first-team place back.

I didn't have to ask. Neath were playing Newport in the quarter-final of the Welsh Cup. Brian Thomas, who during my absence had taken control of the team, wanted me to play.

After only one reserve game? I protested that I wasn't ready, that there was no way I was match-fit, that I hadn't done any kicking practice and that my ball handling was rusty.

Brian was adamant that I was ready. Ron Waldron, the coach who was eventually to run the Welsh team, cut through my arguments by putting his hand on my shoulder and saying: 'Jonathan, it's like farting. Once you've learned you never forget.'

Once more, Trimsaran turned out in force to support me and the game could hardly have gone better for me. I dropped a goal and we won the game. I was named Man of the Match, just as I was after my debut. It had taken me the best part of two years to get back to where I'd started from.

CHAPTER 9

Freedom and Instinct

Jonathan introduced a form of psychological warfare into his game long before he knew what it meant and even longer before he knew how to spell it.

He explains his motives quite simply. 'Opponents always intimidated me by bashing me up. My only way of intimidating them has been to ruffle their confidence, to make them annoyed and ruin their concentration. Mind you, if they get really nasty I do know how to look after myself.'

It was as a puny kid that he first developed what some might think is an arrogant approach. But those who grew up with him recognize that his cheekiness was based on an early decision to make up in bravado for what he lacked in bulk. They would forgive his mocking laugh when he sent them sprawling in the wrong direction, because it was playful. Strangers would not take to it so kindly, especially when he was playing among the seniors in West Wales rugby. They would roll their sleeves higher to make sure they got him next time.

Once he established that a roused temper was easier to confuse, Jonathan built up a repertoire of antics designed to raise the ire and lower the efficiency of the opposition.

It was a perilous approach but a rewarding one. Many a rampaging wing-forward, revelling in his job to clatter the outside half, would throw a practised snarl in the direction of his target only to find himself being blown a kiss and given a saucy wink. The resulting charge to get to grips with this cocky little upstart often lost enough in sense and calculation to increase Jonathan's elusiveness.

He has paraded these tricks at the highest level. John Jeffrey, the Scottish and British Lions wing-forward, was once reduced to incoherent rage trying to capture the little Welshman and make him suffer for his cheek.

Peter Winterbottom, the great England flanker, said after he retired that he had taken on 33 outside halves around the world and the only one he hadn't been able to tackle was Jonathan. 'I played against him four times in internationals,' he said, 'and I never got near him. He was a class above the rest. He could beat anyone, anywhere.'

After one abortive mission, Winterbottom complained to his quarry while they were having an after-match drink: 'It is my job to intimidate you, not the other way round.'

Some didn't get off with merely having faces pulled at them. Mark Jones, the giant Neath back-row man, tried to do a dance on his former team-mate while he lay on the bottom of a ruck. In the course of this intricate footwork, Jones's boot came off. Jonathan sportingly retrieved it and held it out to Jones. As the big man reached gratefully for it, Jonathan threw it into the crowd.

Mike Skinner was another England flanker who regarded himself as a scourge of fly-halves. He caught Jonathan with a thump during Wales's visit to Twickenham in 1987. The next time he tried his arms caught thin air as the outside half vanished from his grasp with an ease that left him time to shout 'Ta ta' over his shoulder as he went on a looping run that set up a try that helped to seal Wales's victory.

Even in the less forgiving ferocity of rugby league, Jonathan was prone to wind up opponents. His intention was merely to put them in two minds. He has long realized that doubt is an enemy in the intensity of a game, and if he can plant a bit of that, he will. He will indicate to the opposing full-back that he intends to favour him with an up and under after the next tackle. Why give a warning?

Most players react instinctively to moves but Jonathan's theory is that if you warn them in advance, they have time to worry about it and a sliver of doubt is often enough. He can threaten opponents with all manner of devilish ploys, just to make them wary. But, then, the whole nature of his game is designed to get the fear of the unpredictable on his side. He has made a habit of inflicting the unexpected since his earliest rugby days.

Meirion Davies, his Trimsaran Primary School mentor, recalls: 'I once saw him attempt to kick the ball downfield, miss the ball deliberately, catch it and run through the astonished opposition to score. *I always wanted to see him do that against England. It was that ability to do something unexpected that marked him out even as a boy. It was what Wales missed most when he changed codes.'*

In league, where they are less inclined to forgive frivolities, Jonathan tried many variations that were appreciated only because they came off, and then grudgingly. Playing against Keighley in 1994 he was hailed as Warrington's hero after winning the match with a try and conversion in the dying seconds. But he was admonished for trying a solo run down the wing on first tackle. He ran into touch, which was tantamount to giving the ball away. The fact that he shouldn't have done it was the reason, of course, that he tried it. He then persuaded Warrington's young stand-off Francis Maloney to kick over the scrum to take the Keighley backs by surprise. It didn't work. Jonathan admitted it was his fault, but Maloney was reprimanded anyway.

It was this quality of unpredictability that first drew him to the attention of Brian Thomas. An outstanding second-row forward in the Sixties, Thomas played for Cambridge, Neath and Wales and had a reputation for a robust and uncompromising style that was carried over into his team management techniques. He had, however, an eye for skill and a desire to see it expressed in his team.

Once or twice he clashed with Jonathan over their tactical approach, but in building Neath into arguably the best club team in Britain during the Eighties he also set the platform for his outside half's rapid rise.

When Jonathan made his debut for Neath in 1982, Thomas was just a spectator. He had yet to be called upon to take charge of the club and revitalize their fortunes. But he took keen note of the frail youngster.

'I had first seen him some time before in a Welsh Youth trial match when he was overlooked in favour of someone else,' remembers Thomas. 'But I had him chalked up in my mind straight away. He looked the part because he had that slick, arrogant air about him. He wanted to take charge.

'Then I saw him again in that first match at the Gnoll and there it was again – the unmistakable look of a player who knows what he wants to do and does it. It was amazing that no one else had picked him out.'

Thomas was appointed team manager of Neath that summer and set about re-organizing the club, delegating specific duties to his two coaches and captain and planning a style of play based on fast, hard-working, ball-winning forwards and a pair of creative half-backs.

Jonathan had a key part to play in that scheme, but his injury in the Snelling Sevens was an early set-back to Thomas, who was not pleased. He said: 'Jonathan has a passion for showing off that is well served by sevens rugby. It appeals to the extrovert in him. But a twisted knee trying something special cost him and us more than 18 months of his career.'

Thomas proceeded with the job of re-shaping Neath and found in Ben Childs an outside half fully capable of responding to the team's requirements. But although Neath made impressive progress in Jonathan's absence, the manager never forgot the extra dimension he felt the youngster could add.

As soon as he reappeared from the injury list, Thomas wanted him in his team. He was certain that Jonathan, by then 21, could step straight into a Welsh Cup quarter-final even though his previous first-class experience amounted to three games more than 18 months earlier and he had tested his fitness in only one reserve match.

Thomas's faith proved to be well founded. The local newspaper described Jonathan's display 'as outstanding a performance as anyone can remember from a fly-half'.

Ken Davies recalls the thrill that ran through the whole club, not just at the way he played that day but because of what it promised for the future: 'If anyone doubted that he was a natural, that one game would have convinced them. He had been out of rugby for over 18 months and yet walked out to take control of the match like a veteran. Brian Thomas had already created a very good side; Jonathan was to be the icing on the cake.'

Although much of Jonathan's appeal revolved around his instinct, his feel for the spontaneous lunge that would rip a hole through the opposition, Brian Thomas saw far more to him. A firm believer in the team ethic, Thomas rated the player as the best outside half he has ever seen because he was the most complete.

'He is the top in my estimation because he was as effective in defence as he was in attack. You put speed, skill, guts and

confidence together and you have a great player. But he had
something else not normally found in that position. He was mean,
sometimes even nasty. He may look vulnerable, but he can be
nasty when it comes to looking after himself and that is a vital
weapon to have when you are as good as he is.'

His team-mates in Trimsaran would not disagree with that
assessment. One of them played with his father, Len, and was still
in the team when Jonathan first appeared. 'I don't know where
Jonathan gets his aggression from, but it wasn't his father. Len
was a terrific player but he didn't have a nasty bone in his body.
Jonathan is different – he won't put up with any nonsense.'

Others who played with him tell of how he would exact
retribution for any brutal treatment in such a subtle way that
it would be noticed by no one except the recipient. It is relatively
easy, for instance, for a player of impeccable timing to arrange a
kick downfield so that the boot has reached an inconvenient
height just as an onrushing opponent reaches him.

Brian Thomas saw that aggressive spirit as an essential strength,
and there were times when it clashed with Brian's own qualities of
that nature. It ensured that their relationship, which was always
strong and mutually respectful, was not always smooth and sweet.

Their closeness was reflected when Jonathan was made club
captain at the age of 23, by which time Brian acknowledged that
there was little about which Jonathan needed guidance when he
went on to the pitch. Not that it would have been easy to make
him listen.

'The only thing you had to harness was his kicking,' says
Thomas. 'He always wanted to keep the ball in play even when
there were occasions when it would have paid to put it into touch.
I never really persuaded him. There were times when he thought it
necessary to kick it out, but he would much prefer to keep it alive,
to put the full-back under pressure. He had the knack of doing that
which few others have.'

When Arwel Thomas arrived in spectacular fashion into the
Welsh outside-half spot just after my return, I was asked if I
would give him some advice following his successful debut against
Italy. We watched a video of the match together and I pointed out
one or two things.

I felt a little awkward. Not because of him. He is a great lad and comes from the same sort of West Wales village background that I do. I also interviewed him on radio in my new role with the BBC and we got along very well.

The reason I felt awkward, apart from the fact that he was in the shirt I wanted, was that I know only too well how difficult it is for an instinctive player to take advice. Trying to explain the sort of pressure he would be facing in the forthcoming international against England at Twickenham and advising him how to cope was fair enough, but I found it very difficult to go much further because I know how I would have reacted in his place.

There are outside halves – too many these days, I fear – who can be programmed how to play, how to react to this or that situation, but my sort, and I suspect Arwel's, prefer not to have their minds cluttered up with pre-arranged plays.

It is wrong to think I would never listen to advice. I wouldn't be so rude. You can learn by listening to others and I never rejected any advice out of hand. Whether I took any notice is another matter. It is hard to tell. You may absorb some suggestions subconsciously and they may surface in your play at some later stage, but although I have learned many things from many people I'm not aware of having learned anything about outside-half play from anyone. I just go out and do what I think is best for the team and what we are trying to achieve at any particular time.

If I was going to listen to anyone I would have listened to my father, but I didn't have to. He had the wisdom to realize that advice is meaningless if you haven't got the ability to put it into practice. And if you have the ability, you don't need the advice.

He made sure only that I built up a relationship with any and every type of ball and encouraged me to do what my instincts told me to do. I think it is significant that many of the things I did at the peak of my union career had first come into my head when I was 11 or under.

I approached every stepping stone in my career with the same attitude, with nothing clouding my brain except anxiety about how I was going to fare. The more challenges I met and overcame, the more my confidence grew. But I never let that confidence turn into arrogance.

If all this suggests that I owe nothing to anyone then I am insulting many people. Rugby is a team game; more than that, it is a club game. On and off the field, so many minds and bodies are involved that it is almost presumptuous for a player to think of his efforts and achievements in a personal way. But if the best service you can do for the team and club is to let your instinct rule your reaction to a situation, then you must do it. The quality of those around you will decide how much tolerance your instinct will be granted. I would have achieved nothing without my team-mates.

When I went to rugby league it was a while before I dared let my instincts rule my actions. It is a game in which skill can flourish, but it has a strict discipline about what to do in certain situations. When I challenged that and did something totally unexpected, I was judged purely on what I had achieved. That's the professional approach and I appreciated it. Whenever I failed, the wrath of my team-mates had to be faced. The more successes my unorthodox play achieved, the more tolerant they became at my occasional failures, but it is not easy trying to be spontaneous in either code these days . . .

I recall only one occasion during my time at Neath when Brian Thomas tried to put a rein on my instinctive play. We were in the dressing-room at Bridgend, where we were about to play a very hard game.

Brian said to me: 'Jonathan, whenever you get the ball I want you to bang it as far downfield as you can.'

I said: 'I'm sorry, Brian, I'll decide what to do when I get the ball. I'll play it as I see fit.'

'Never mind about all that,' he shouted, 'I want it in their half!'

I took off my shirt and offered it to him. 'Do you want this?' I demanded.

'Do you want a broken nose?' he asked.

I put the shirt back on and, strangely enough, I did put in quite a few long touch kicks. But I did so because that's what my instinct told me to do at the time. The boys might have thought I was merely obeying orders, but Brian had rightly predicted what our game would require – I didn't know until I got out there!

The downfall of many an outside half, and perhaps the reason the game hasn't got too many creative ones, is not that they lack ability but that they get their heads full of so many orders and tactical priorities that their natural instincts get pushed into the background. Every time they receive the ball they have to pause that vital split second before they decide what to do. Too often, that hesitation allows the opposition to close down most of the options.

I am certain that many players in all forms of football suffer because they are asked to conform to a strict tactical pattern. Of course, every team needs to have a basic structure of play, but it must be flexible, otherwise we get the sterile and boring exhibitions we've seen too often in all codes.

I would prefer not to play the game than have my mind conditioned to act in a pre-defined way. And I certainly wouldn't watch a game in which I felt the players were laced into a system that frowned on individuality.

It is possible for any match to develop a period of stalemate, but as long as I know that there are players out there who have the skill and the freedom to use it I will watch and wait patiently for that moment of magic that makes sport so worthwhile. And as long as I am playing I will continually seek that moment when I can produce a move that changes the flow of the game in favour of my team and gives me the great satisfaction of creating something from nothing.

Whether I would have been able to build a career on the basis of my ability to do the unexpected if I hadn't entered the first-class game under Brian Thomas's influence is to be doubted. He played a major part in my development purely because he was keen for me to express myself. Had I gone to another club, it is probable that my natural urges would have been suppressed in favour of a more orthodox approach. Perhaps that explains why the outside-half factory has been seriously under-producing for several years – club coaches have been unwilling to let players run free.

The safety-first approach presumes that an adventurous style is risky. That is ridiculous. Winning has always been the prime objective. Brian instilled that in me. He just happened to believe that creating a team framework in which players could freely use their talents was the best way to win. I've never seen sense in any other approach, and the only time I would do anything purposely negative is to preserve a winning situation for the team.

The policy requires considerable confidence from yourself and those around you. The trouble is that I never know what I'm going to do until I've done it. People have talked about my speed off the mark, but what they don't realize is that the fastest thing off the mark is my brain. That's why I don't want it cluttered up with instructions.

My instinct decides the best option even as the ball is coming into my hands. I've gained a yard on the opposition before my feet have moved. Being positive about what I am going to do is the main fuel for my surges. It is amazing how much quicker you can be if you know exactly where you are going.

This may sound fanciful, but sometimes I've set off even before my brain has caught up with where my instinct is aiming me. It is a most exciting feeling and I often get as much thrill as the crowd, because it is as much a surprise to me that I've found a gap as it is to them. And if I seem highly delighted about it, it's not arrogance but simply the pleasure of the experience. After all, if everyone else can enjoy it, why can't I?

That's why my comeback was so special. I didn't believe I could do it. Brian did, but he still took an enormous chance in playing me so soon. If only other coaches had shown such faith in me . . . He didn't even give me any instructions before the game; nor a pep-talk. He just murmured a few words of encouragement and I went out and put my trust in my ability.

From then on it was a fairy tale for someone who had been away from the game for 18 months. Because Neath operated a strict squad system I didn't play in every match, but I was there when we beat Aberavon in the semi-final. We were to play Cardiff in the final at the National Stadium, and I still hadn't played in more than a dozen first-class matches.

My life off the pitch was also beginning to take shape. Karen and I had become engaged in May 1982 when we were both 19. She was watching me play in the Snelling Sevens when I suffered the knee injury and spent the next 18 months consoling a very miserable fiancé.

By then Karen had qualified as a medical technician and worked in the laboratory at Glangwili Hospital where I had my knee operation. We were saving to get married, but although I had come to the end of my three-year apprenticeship I was still earning only £90 a week.

Then I saw an advertisement for labourers at the Ffos Las opencast coalmine, a few hundred yards from my home. The pay was £140 a week but that wasn't the main attraction. Wimpey, the owners, were guaranteeing security of employment at the mine for 25 years. Security was not a word often to be heard in a place like Trimsaran. Those who have never known insecurity will not appreciate why I had to take that job.

To the surprise of everyone I became a banksman at the mine, where my duties included keeping the fleet of bulldozers topped up with oil and water and cleaning the mud off them at the end of the day. The hours were awful – 6 a.m. to 7 p.m. every weekday and 6 a.m. to 12 noon on Saturdays.

I didn't mind the work, but after removing great lumps of mud from the front blades of the bulldozers and from between the treads of the tyres I'd jump straight into Ken's car to go to Neath for training. I used to go into the club afterwards and fall fast asleep in the bar without the aid of any alcohol.

I stuck it for three months and then confessed to Brian Thomas that the job was beginning to affect my rugby. Perhaps it would be better if I went back to playing for Trimsaran, because I needed that job, hard as it was. Men who do that sort of work all their lives have my admiration.

Brian's reaction was to start seeking alternative employment for me, and an industrialist friend of his called Neil O'Halloran arranged an interview for me at a painting and shot-blasting firm. By that time I had passed my driving test at the third attempt and paid £300 for an old Morris Marina, so I was able to relieve Ken of the chore of ferrying me around. Three times I had to drive down to Cardiff for interviews before I finally clinched the job.

The pay was about the same as at Ffos Las, but there were fewer hours, a car was provided and there wasn't a bulldozer in sight. I was putting aside the dungarees and becoming a white-collar worker. It has been said that Welsh rugby started to go downhill when players forsook manual work for softer jobs. I don't know if the theory is right but, even if it is, it shouldn't apply to outside halves.

My new task was to tour the contracts we were undertaking in various parts of West Wales to make sure our painters were happy and that the customers had no complaints. I also helped to get new business and give a hand with the estimating.

I enjoyed the work but I had no illusions about why I was there. It wasn't because I was an expert on painting. The firm was part of the group of companies owned by Neil O'Halloran, who loved sport and was quite a sporting celebrity himself. He was a very good soccer player who played for Cardiff City and made history by scoring a hat-trick on his debut against Charlton Athletic.

A boilermaker by trade, he built up an impressive industrial empire in South Wales but, thankfully, never lost his passion for sport. Soccer remained his first love, and before his sadly premature death in 1995 he had built Barry Town into one of Wales's leading clubs.

I was the second rugby player he employed. The first was the great Terry Holmes, by then well established as the Welsh scrum-half. I already idolized him as a player and now enjoyed knowing him as a colleague and a friend. For the first time in my life everything was progressing smoothly. Having a job made me more relaxed and self-assured, and I learned a great deal from Neil, just as I did from Brian Thomas, about how to conduct myself, have faith in my ability, sum people up and sort out the goodies from the baddies. For a 21-year-old, it was a university course in itself.

I hope Neil felt I was worth the trouble. I really did try to make a contribution but, let's face it, Terry and I were there because we were well-known rugby players, Terry much more than me. We weren't earning a fortune, certainly nowhere near as much as comparable players in certain other countries, but you could class us as professionals in that we were making a living out of being rugby union players.

The rugby establishment, of course, were quite happy that someone else was looking after us. They could enjoy their privileged, if not luxurious, place as the proud rulers of amateur rugby as long as someone else paid their players.

When all was considered, I counted myself lucky. Players either fended for themselves, had the good fortune to find a keen employer, or struggled to keep their place in an amateur game in which only professionals could succeed.

Working with Terry, of course, made it all the more exciting that I would be playing against him in the Schweppes Welsh Cup

Final. Neath had made great strides under Brian but we were the definite underdogs against the might of Cardiff who, besides Terry, had another hero of mine, Gareth Davies, at outside half, plus the great lock Bob Norster, the England captain John Scott, and two brilliant Welsh backs in Mark Ring and Adrian Hadley.

Cardiff were probably the most formidable team in Britain at that time, while Neath were still in the early stages of Thomas's revolution. One extra treat for me was that another Trimsaran boy, Carl Bridgewater, had earned a place in the Neath team. There were hardly enough wheels in West Wales to transport the Trimsaran contingent to Cardiff.

I'm afraid the occasion got the better of me. Probably over-awed by playing opposite the reigning Welsh outside half, I rushed at Gareth as he was making a kick early in the game and hit him with a late tackle. It probably didn't hurt him one bit, but as I trotted back to my position, Terry Holmes said quietly: 'That's enough of that now, Jon.'

I took the rebuke and never thought of repeating the act. In fact, I hurt myself because he left his foot up and I had six stud marks down my chest. It is a trick I used to protect myself later in my career.

In the end we lost 26–19 and made a good game of it. This was the big time, and I had enjoyed my first taste of it.

CHAPTER 10

Welsh Dream Comes True

If Jonathan's progress into first-class rugby was slow, sometimes painfully so, the speed of his advancement from then on was exceptionally quick. Where previously barriers had sprung up to impede him, now the path to the game's high peaks opened up before him like the Red Sea before Moses.

If you take his February 1984 comeback to the Neath side as the real starting date of his career in the top flight, he won his way into the Welsh team after only 14 months and a total of 35 games – and during that time he had graduated via the accepted route of membership of the Welsh squad, a 'B' international and a place on the replacements bench.

It was as if his guardian angel had suddenly reported for duty and was determined to make up for lost time. Although Jonathan continued to attract the eye in the improving Neath team, there were a few other fly-halves ahead of him in the queue for national consideration. Entry into the Welsh team, however, is subject to the whims of fate more than most and Jonathan benefited from a highly fortunate chain of events.

Wales were due to begin their Five Nations Championship programme in 1985 with a match against England at Cardiff, but it was postponed because of bad weather and put back until 20 April. Wales then played Scotland at Murrayfield, where they won 25–21. The following match was at Cardiff, where Wales lost 21–9 to the eventual champions, Ireland. Then came the visit to Paris, where Wales lost to France 14–3.

The irony is that had the game against England been played on its original date and had Wales won, as they usually did in those days, they might well have gone on to have a more successful championship and would have felt no need to change the team. As it was, they became undecided what to do for the England game.

Occupying the outside-half position was Gareth Davies, who had been restored to the team that season. He had been captain of Wales previously and starred in the ill-fated game against England which Wales nearly won despite having had Paul Ringer sent off. But Gareth was dropped after Wales lost 34–18 to Scotland at Cardiff in 1982. Swansea's Malcolm Dacey took over the position for the next two seasons until he in turn lost the place back to Gareth.

What happened then is still remembered as a notorious decision. The Welsh selectors announced three new caps in the team to play England but put the name A.N. Other in the outside-half spot. They explained that they wanted to take another look at the candidates. Even by their standards, this was a monstrous piece of insensitivity. Gareth Davies had 21 caps for Wales. If they didn't know what he was capable of by then, they never would.

It so happened that Cardiff were playing Swansea that Saturday. As the main contenders, Gareth and Dacey were virtually playing for the vacancy in the Welsh team. Gareth decided it was a situation in which he wanted no part. He immediately took the only honourable course of action open to him: he announced his retirement from international rugby.

When Saturday came, Gareth was given a tremendous reception by the Cardiff crowd when he ran on to the field. To the further delight of the Cardiff supporters he then proceeded to give a brilliant display that completely outclassed Dacey's offering. Had he not retired, Gareth would almost certainly have been chosen to continue as the Welsh No. 10 and, at the age of 31, might have occupied the place for another season or two. But that wasn't to be, and they could hardly recall Dacey.

Jonathan, meanwhile, was playing for Neath against Gloucester at the Gnoll where the Welsh coach John Bevan (later to succumb to a fatal illness) and a couple of selectors saw him play a typically audacious game. Playing into a strong wind in the first half, Neath benefited from Jonathan's adventurous kicking to take a half-time lead which he helped to maintain with a try-saving tackle in the second half.

Next morning Rod Morgan, chairman of the selectors, telephoned. 'Congratulations, Jonathan,' he said, 'you have been selected to play against England.'

Jonathan hesitated. He remembered that Rod had used exactly the same words a few weeks earlier when he rang to tell him he was on the replacements bench for the French match. 'As replacement?' he asked. 'No, outside half,' was the reply.

The tears broke out as soon as I put down the phone and told my mother I had been picked for Wales. The joy, combined with the thought of how proud my father would have been, was too potent a weeping mixture to resist. And the tears flowed even more freely when I rang Karen with the news. Her father Byron had died suddenly only a matter of days earlier, and it had been his ambition to see me play for Wales.

Karen's dad had been ill ever since I had known her. He suffered from kidney trouble and when we were first courting he was spending hours every day on a dialysis machine installed at the back of the house. It was a tedious and unpleasant procedure, but we used to help and spend as much time as we could with him. He eventually had a kidney transplant and made an excellent recovery. Eight months after he gave Karen away at our wedding he collapsed and died of a heart attack while we were all having a meal. He was 49 and we were still in a state of shock.

Fortunately, we were given no time to dwell on how unkind the family fates had been. The word of my selection soon got around and in no time the house was full of well-wishers. Eventually the party transferred itself to Trimsaran Rugby Club, where we were to be joined by two coachloads from Neath, including Brian Thomas and Ken Davies, who'd come to help us celebrate.

We were a little short of local support. The Trimsaran Over-35s team had left early that morning to play in Gloucester and after the match were happily installed in the home team's clubhouse. My stepfather Ken, no longer a player but a keen social member, was with them and was at the bar when two policemen walked in. Since it was Sunday and stop-tap had long since passed there was a respectful hush. One of the policemen shouted: 'If there's anyone from Trimsaran Rugby Club here we have a message that somebody called Jonathan has been chosen for Wales.'

It was 5 o'clock before someone suggested it would be a good idea to continue the party back home. They got thirsty before they reached Trimsaran and called in for one at the British Legion in

Loughor. They were still there at 10 o'clock when Ken took an irate call from the Trimsaran chairman Hywel 'Titch' Richards complaining that the clubhouse was packed with Neath fans celebrating with Jonathan while the bulk of the Trimsaran club were still not back from a morning fixture.

As soon as I saw Ken, of course, I burst into tears again. He was the only senior male member of my family to have survived to see my dreams realized. The party went on till near daybreak and I didn't go to work next morning.

I was one of four new caps. The others were the centre Kevin Hopkins, Phil Davies at No. 8 and Gareth Roberts, the wing-forward. Terry Holmes, of course, was scrum-half and captain and I couldn't have asked for a better half-back partner to nurse me through my international debut. I've been very lucky with scrum-halves. My early days at Neath had been made much easier by having Carl Cnojeck as a playing partner. Carl came from Resolven and was of Polish extraction. He was only five feet tall but he was a super player and, apart from showing me how beer should be drunk, never gave me a bad ball. He gave it quickly, too, so that I always had that extra yard.

Among Terry's many talents was the ability to give a long pass that is so vital for an outside half who is looking for that extra split second to try something different. He is also a very calm and strong character, and when I arrived at the Arms Park for the England game I was grateful for the steady reassurance of a friend. 'Just go out and play your own game,' he insisted as I fussed and fretted about in the dressing-room. Our coach, John Bevan, also encouraged me to follow my instinct and added that if I was going to kick to make sure I put the opposition under pressure.

What I was not expecting was the impact of the occasion. Millions of words have been written about the mystic *hwyl*, the battle spirit that takes over a man when he puts on the red shirt of Wales. I suspect that even the Welsh take it with a pinch of salt. I think I did, too, until it happened to me. It really is like having a psychological power-pack strapped to your back.

Although every detail of my first international is still vivid in my memory, what I remember most is the team spirit that day. It was the most powerful I'd ever come cross. The setting, the crowd and the red shirt bring a great deal of fervour to you, but it was something about the feeling among the team that impressed me more than anything. It was genuinely uplifting and it just drove my nerves away. Obviously, I was much younger then and more impressionable, but that feeling was not so intense when I played my last game three years later. I came to the conclusion that during even that brief time the Welsh spirit lost some of its power to inspire.

But it was certainly present on that day, and just as well. Whatever the situation, beating England is always its own priority but it meant more that day because we had lost to France and Ireland and only narrowly defeated the wooden spoonists Scotland. We had also lost the previous four games at the Arms Park, and if England won, we would have created a new record in Welsh failure. Despite this added pressure, our *hwyl* was such that defeat didn't seem a remote possibility. We were so full of confidence that even a 50-yard penalty from Rob Andrew in the first minute didn't worry us. I imagine the other new caps were particularly encouraged, as I was, by the way experienced players like Terry Holmes, Bob Norster and John Perkins attacked the game with such bite and enthusiasm.

My Neath team-mate Paul Thorburn had won his way into the Welsh team in the previous game against France and we were to need his accurate kicking. Paul equalized Andrew's early penalty, but then England scored a try through Simon Smith which Andrew converted.

I did plenty of kicking because I felt my best policy was to keep driving the English pack back. The fact that Rob was trying just as hard to drive them forward made it a very interesting battle. Paul kicked two more penalties to level the score again, but Rob struck again just before half-time to edge them ahead once more.

The referee was looking at his watch and we were in injury time when I got my name on the score-sheet. We had forced our way close and I received the ball from a scrum, fairly close in but with little time, and dropped a goal. The ball only just crept over the bar, but it counted and we were level at a vital time.

Rob Andrew played well that day. He was certainly determined not to be upstaged by this little upstart and dropped a goal left-footed at the start of the second half to make it 15–12 in England's favour. But our forwards were beginning to get the upper hand in their tough battle with the English pack, and the break we had been looking for came when I hoisted a high kick towards the England line. Even as the ball left my boot I cursed because I had overdone it. Instead of hovering in the air and dropping into the vulnerable area 15 yards in front of the line, the ball was arcing towards the English full-back Chris Martin.

I was praised afterwards for following up so quickly, but my one thought was to get up there to retrieve what I could from my cock-up. But, under pressure from Robert Ackerman, Martin made a mess of catching the ball. It spun out of his grasp and right into my path and all I had to do was to pounce on the ball to score my first try in international rugby.

It was a blow from which England never recovered and towards the end of play I managed to set up a move that was finished off by Gareth Roberts and we came off 24–15 winners. The elation, not to mention the relief, was felt all over Wales.

I was criticized then and later for being too belligerent towards Rob Andrew, for trying to knock his head off in international matches. But if I ever went in hard against him it was only part of the hurly-burly of the game. I don't recall him being particularly gentle towards me. But we were rivals, after all. I have never felt any personal animosity towards Rob and we've always got on well off the field. The fact that I still feel guilty whenever I meet him is to do with something that happened after that game.

As we came off the field I agreed with Rob, as is traditional, to exchange shirts. I asked him to wait until afterwards. In the dressing-room, I had the Welsh shirt I wore on the replacements bench in the previous game. It had No. 16 on the back. I gave it to him with the number hidden as he gave me his match shirt in return. It was a desperately sneaky thing to do. In my defence I must say that I was worried that it might have been my first and last game for Wales. I desperately wanted to treasure that No. 10 shirt in case it was my last. I went home to the Trimsaran celebrations next day with both the No. 10 shirts.

Rob has had the decency never to mention the incident, but perhaps he will be more inclined to forgive me when I reveal that after a match against Scotland a year or two later, I gave my shirt to their outside half who had been making his debut, and refused to take his in exchange. I said that as it was his first he should keep it – like I had kept mine!

My happy memories of my debut are not contradicted by the newspaper cuttings I've kept. A debut boy scoring twice was good stuff for the headlines and one or two newspapers named me Man of the Match. I knew how lucky I had been with the try but, then again, I'd been asked to put the opposition under pressure and that's what I did. It is a corny expression that you make your own luck, but there is a strong element of truth in it. I've tried too many things that have failed unluckily not to feel justified in accepting praise for one that went my way.

As for worrying about the supply of red shirts coming to a sudden end, I was selected for the next game which was against Fiji later in the year. This turned out to be a sad occasion. It was to be Terry Holmes's last game for Wales. Not long after it, he announced his decision to turn professional with Bradford Northern. I was to lose a friend, a colleague and the best scrum-half partner a young international could ask for.

I suppose Terry's departure first sowed the seeds of league in my mind. At the time, I didn't have the slightest interest. Everything was happening for me in union. But spending so much time with Terry and having had long conversations about rugby and its effect on our lives, it was natural that I would regard him as a role model. We came from similar working-class backgrounds and knew how lucky we were to find an employer like Neil. But what about the long-term future?

It was a shock for me when he left. At the age of 28 he was the hero of Cardiff, one of the greatest clubs in the world, captain of Wales and an established British Lion. And here he was turning his back on all that and leaving his beloved home city in order to get some tangible reward from his rugby before it was too late. He had achieved things in rugby that even someone as ambitious as I didn't dare dream about, and in the end he had to pack his bags and leave in order to earn some financial security for his family. It didn't seem right and it troubled me.

There was no time for me to get unsettled. Since that first match against England, doors were opening to places I never knew had doors. For a start, that summer Neath made me their captain. I was 22 years of age and the youngest captain in the club's history.

What made it all the more difficult to grasp was that the captain I replaced was Elgan Rees, the man who had nursed me through my early days with the club a couple of years before. Elgan had relinquished the job because he felt a younger player should have a go, and he was delighted it was me.

Before I led Neath into the next season, I was invited to join the famous Scottish invitation side, the Co-optimists, who were touring Zimbabwe. Suddenly I was flying to Africa in the company of players like the legendary Irish forward Moss Keane, who tried to learn to swim on that trip but found that alcohol was not the best aid to keeping 19 stone afloat. While we were in Zimbabwe we visited a safari park where our coach stopped in the lion compound for us to get out and walk around. We were told the lions were quite tame but suddenly one of them attacked a little boy who was there with his parents. Before the lion could do any harm Hugh McHardy ran up and kicked the lion so hard it turned its attention on us. The sight of 30 rugby players trying to get back into a coach at the same time must be fresh in those lions' minds even now.

After the Co-optimists, I was invited to play in a World Sevens tournament in South Africa in a team that included the Australians David Campese, Glen Ella and Roger Gould. Once more I was in illustrious company and my eyes were getting wider by the day. But I was brought face to face with apartheid for the first and, I made sure, the last time. I walked into a crowded bar with Glen Ella and we were about to start jostling our way through when the crowd parted as if by magic. We got to the bar with ease. Then it dawned on me – Glen is an aborigine, and we were experiencing the opposite of a warm welcome. We got merrily pissed together, almost as an act of defiance.

I then had an experience in Durban which left another painful memory of the place. I was in some distress and discomfort from piles and went to a doctor for help. I was thinking about some cream, but he went to work with a scalpel without bothering with an anaesthetic.

These were the stories with which I regaled the Trimsaran clubhouse on my return. They were suitably absorbed by my adventures and my name-dropping, but I was careful not to get too clever. I had already received a lesson in humility from my fellow villagers.

Before I joined Neath, I conducted most of my life, at home, at work and on the rugby pitch, in the Welsh language. I tend to chatter a lot when I'm playing, which was fine in the Trimsaran team in which everybody spoke Welsh, but at Neath I had to speak in English. Elgan Rees and the farmers like Kevin Phillips and Brian Williams spoke Welsh but, since the rest didn't, English was the common language of the team. I found it hard to get used to at first, but since I was also travelling further afield with my work I was using English more than ever.

Just before we played Cardiff in the Welsh Cup Final I was interviewed on a Welsh language sports programme. It was my first time on TV and I preened myself as the interviewer asked me: 'Sut wyt ti'n teimlio?' (How do you feel?) I told him exactly. 'It is a dream come true,' I answered proudly. Then I stared at him in horror. I'd replied in English. Instead of saying 'Breuddwyd wedi dod yn wir,' the flush of the moment had turned my words.

I mean no offence to the English language, but I was brought up in Welsh and that is the language of my home. If we are in the company of those who only speak English, then we speak English. But it is our second language and still has the reputation of being the posh language.

For me to use English at a time like that was to exhibit airs and graces well above my station. When I got back to the club that evening, I was hoping no one had seen the television. But as I walked through the door everybody started chanting, 'Dream come true, dream come true . . .' I still haven't lived it down. It was not seen as the act of a humble man.

I have always relied upon Trimsaran to keep my feet on the ground. They were hard pushed to do that over the next couple of years.

CHAPTER 11

Out of Order

The ability and resilience to meet the challenges that both codes throughout the world have regularly flung in Jonathan's face were largely acquired in a stretch of brilliance on the rugby field – and trouble off it – that was remarkable by any sportsman's standards. While the years 1986 and 1987 established him as a world-wide star, they also revealed a flair for controversy that ensured he didn't need a rugby match to create a headline.

Every plaudit for a style of play that grew more and more outstanding seemed to be accompanied by a problem that threatened to remove him from the stabilizing forces of his life. He fell out, in a series of highly publicized fractures, with his wife Karen, the Welsh Rugby Union, his mentor Brian Thomas and the police in a whirl of activity he seemed unable to control.

In May 1986 he was voted British Player of the Year by the readers of Rugby World. *His surging, inventive play not only embellished the performances of Neath and Wales but made him ideal for sevens rugby and highly suitable for those select invitation teams who love to play open and adventurous rugby. An impish genius is rugby's favourite animal, and the breed had become a rarity, almost extinct.*

That year, he travelled a total of 80,000 miles to earn global recognition of his talent. In any other major sport, and in most walks of life, these demands for his services would have earned him a considerable amount of money. All they did earn him were rebukes from those who feared he might burn himself out.

It is difficult to reason with a young man who suddenly finds himself the centre of attraction. He received flattering requests from touring teams like the Scottish Co-optimists, the Irish Wolfhounds and the Barbarians. He grabbed every challenge

131

on offer and made a success of them, especially that which was probably the hardest: being captain of Neath at such a tender age.

To the qualities that Brian Thomas had recognized years earlier, he added positive leadership. The exploitation of the half-gap, the astute tactical kicking, the defensive covering and tackling were topped by the ability to inspire those around him.

A typical scene was portrayed by John Billot of the Western Mail *in his report of a match between Neath and Abertillery. Neath were leading by just 4–3 after half-an-hour of dour stuff. During an injury stoppage the captain decided to administer a pep-talk, and in Billot's words, 'Little Jonathan in the middle of a huddle of hulking forwards could be heard squeakily outlining his requirements – by the end of the game they had scored nine tries.'*

The Neath forwards responded to him because, as pack leader Mike Richards explained at the time, 'Our forwards know that good, hard-won ball is not going to be wasted and that when they win possession they are going to be moving forward with it.'

This attacking style led to a rush of tries from forwards as well as backs. At one time during this period, Neath were averaging four tries a match thanks to Jonathan's imaginative ability to create gaps for those around him.

The only complaint Neath's fans made was that they didn't see enough of him, what with international calls and his globe-trotting. His first full Five Nations Championship that season confirmed his promise. Against Ireland in Dublin, Wales were losing until Jonathan brilliantly created a try that led to victory. At Twickenham, Rob Andrew stole the show by scoring a record 21 points in England's 21–18 victory, but it was Jonathan who caught the connoisseur's eye by cheekily endeavouring to attack from drop-outs from his own 25. He then helped Wales to beat Scotland with blistering runs from deep inside his own half, 'rekindling,' wrote one critic, 'a vitality which many had thought had disappeared into some other world of Celtic mist'.

Perhaps his finest hour came in the Sydney Sevens, where he played in the Welsh team and commandeered most of the praise despite some exalted rivals. New Zealand were the inevitable winners, but Wales took the edge off their triumph by beating them in the qualifying pool early in the tournament. Jonathan scored three tries in 14 minutes – few, if any, had achieved that against the All Blacks in any form of rugby.

Wales also beat France, Tonga and the United States before losing narrowly, and unluckily, to the host nation, Australia, in the semi-finals. Jonathan scored seven tries in all and although there was no official best player's award, he was generally hailed as the revelation of the tournament.

Alan Jones, the Australian coach who made such an impact on world rugby, called him a 'cocky little bugger', which passes for praise in that country. Local television commentators, not usually inclined to lavish praise on Britons, described his tries with words like 'sensational' and 'absolutely dynamic'.

While in Sydney, he had an offer to play for the Irish Wolf-hounds in the Hong Kong Sevens a few weeks later. This involved returning home, playing for the Barbarians against Cardiff on Easter Saturday and then flying back to the Far East. Then he heard he'd been selected for the British Lions to play against the Rest of the World at Twickenham. That was the biggest honour of all – and he missed it through injury.

It was all too much, of course, and brought heavy words of concern from Bleddyn Williams, one of the most respected of all Welsh rugby heroes, who warned in the Sunday People:

'Jonathan Davies can become the greatest fly-half in the world . . . but he must learn to say "No" now and again or he'll disappear even faster than he arrived.'

Bleddyn then went on to describe the itinerary that had begun with the 20,000-mile round trip to Sydney:

'Six days later he was the mastermind as the Barbarians beat Cardiff and then he flew another 15,000 miles to play in the Hong Kong Sevens for an Irish team. It is hardly surprising that a hamstring injury keeps him out of the British Lions v. The Rest match.

'Davies will not spend the summer taking a breather. He'll be off to Fiji, Tonga and Western Samoa as the only fly-half in the Welsh touring party. Wales are relying on the 23-year-old Davies to survive all this and lead them to what could be the start of another golden era.

'There is no doubt he has all the talent and charisma of former heroes Barry John and Phil Bennett. In Australia his superb *performances sent highly critical writers and fans into ecstasies. Mark Ella, the brilliant Australian fly-half who destroyed British rugby last year, was captivated by Davies. Ella is the greatest fly-half of modern times and for him to rave about Davies is praise indeed. But Ella has now retired – far too early – because he was unable to cope with the pressures of today's rugby. He found his private life was non-existent and eventually he became totally disillusioned with the game. That's what "the hottest property in world rugby" must avoid.'*

Although I didn't think so at the time, Bleddyn Williams had it right. I was doing too much, too fast. But I was young and eager, and who was to stop me? That was another drawback of the great amateur code. Because they weren't able to pay you, they couldn't dictate to you. A headstrong young player would lose out both ways. He went without financial reward and discipline. A bright prospect wouldn't be allowed to do it these days. His club and country would have the power to shape his career more sensibly.

I was never short of advice but I was lacking in any sense of needing to listen to it. I took every opportunity as if it would be my last, and those who cautioned me didn't realize that I was engaged in a secret activity that would have appalled them even more. I was consorting with the enemy.

I was having secret meetings with Harry Jepson, the chairman of Leeds Rugby League Club. Harry is a respected and popular figure in rugby league and I soon discovered why. His long association with the game, and with watching union, made him very knowledgeable. He is also extremely likeable and as straight as they come. He became interested in trying to persuade me to move north after watching my debut for Wales against England and kept his eye on me whenever he could get down to South Wales.

We once met in the Ivy Bush Hotel in Carmarthen and he pulled from his pocket a cheque made out to me for £30,000. 'That's just the down payment,' he said. The incident had quite an impact on an impoverished 23-year-old. I'll never forget it. I was eating minestrone soup at the time.

Another time, Harry arrived in Cardiff for a meeting with me and, since he was early, decided to have a look around the Arms

Park. He strolled on to the pitch, where someone asked if they could help him. He explained that he was down from the north and wanted a look at the famous stadium. He was given a conducted tour and, up above the pitch, he could see the WRU secretary, Ray Williams, in his office. Harry wondered if they would have been so hospitable had they known he was trying to entice their outside half away.

Harry was a very persuasive man and was adamant, both to me and his board back at Leeds, that I would be ideal for the league code. I was convinced he was wrong. It had been hard enough for a player of my size to make it in union; it would be impossible in such a physical game as league. I think his colleagues at Leeds might have made the same point, but Harry brushed aside all such suggestions. He cited the case of a Welshman called Oliver Morris from Pontypridd who was the finest outside half he had seen. Oliver weighed 9st 6lbs when he went north in 1937. He was rejected by Warrington, but Harry helped to get him a chance at Hunslet. Oliver was a key figure for Hunslet when they won the championship in 1938. When war broke out, Oliver joined the Welch Regiment and was killed in action. Harry is sure he would have become one of the greats.

Although I was having the time of my life enjoying the glory of my new success in union, Harry's keen interest was making me think hard about my future. That magnetic word security was much in my thoughts. Leeds were offering £100,000 tax free, which for a 23-year-old in 1986 was an extremely attractive lump of money. It was £20,000 more than Terry Holmes was reputed to have received from Bradford Northern a few months earlier.

At the start of the 1986–87 season, Leeds invited me and Karen to pay a visit to the club and have a look around. I wanted to see a rugby league match in the flesh. Although I was an avid viewer of televised matches, I had never seen one close up. There was a Yorkshire Cup tie between Featherstone and Hull KR while we were there and Harry took us down.

Featherstone's Post Office Road ground was packed out and the only accommodation they could give us was in one of their new executive boxes in their rebuilt stand. The box was glass-sided and it was like being in a goldfish bowl. Rugby league folk are no less inquisitive than anyone else, and the directors of both clubs and all the other officials in the stand were craning to see who Harry had with him. He explained later that I was a friend from Australia, but when the match was over he hesitated before taking us into the Portakabin that was serving as a temporary boardroom while the stand was being finished. Harry knew as well as I did that I risked trouble from the WRU just by being at a league match with him.

'All the national press will be in there,' he said. 'They're bound to recognize you.'

I decided not to be bothered by the risk, so we went in and Harry introduced me all round as his friend John. I shook hands with all the reporters, who obviously had no idea who I was and probably felt that anyone my size was hardly likely to be a story.

After I'd signed for Widnes, Harry had great pleasure in informing those same press boys that he was surprised they were making such a fuss about Jonathan Davies when they'd ignored me completely when he'd introduced me to them a few years earlier!

I came so close to signing for Leeds, I often reflect on how my career would have developed. Harry is convinced I would have become an even greater success, but I am not so sure. The three extra years I spent in union helped to mature me and make me more confident both mentally and physically. Had I gone to Leeds in 1986, I could not have placed my future in better hands than Harry's and the club coach Peter Fox. But, at 23, I might not have been as prepared for the demands on my body and my mind as I was at 27.

Once I made my mind up to go to Widnes, Harry was the first person I rang. He was gracious enough to say that I was going to a great club and to wish me all the best.

Meanwhile, it was certainly no hardship to be in union. Brian Thomas and Ron Waldron had got the club buzzing and Neath were fast becoming the team no one in the country relished playing. Our try-scoring rate was tremendous, thanks to the pack winning so much good ball I was free to take several options every time I got the ball.

Losing Terry Holmes as my scrum-half and mentor in the Welsh team proved not to be a hardship for too long. When the Five Nations came around in 1986, I was teamed up with a new scrum-half, Robert Jones of Swansea, who was to become a firm friend and a brilliant partner in 25 internationals.

When Wales decided to enter a team in the inaugural Sydney Sevens I was delighted. Brian Thomas always said I liked sevens rugby because it gave me a chance to show off. I'm not sure about that. I just like running with the ball, and sevens gives you plenty of chance for that.

Considering it was our first attempt at sevens as a nation, we did very well to reach the semi-final in which we were narrowly beaten by Australia. But it was a great two days and I came out of it with far more world-wide recognition than I had before.

I also learned a great deal from watching great players at work. I particularly remember Serge Blanco, the great French full-back. When we played France, I noticed that Serge was following my positioning on the field. If I appeared at centre, so did he. If I popped up on the wing, he was opposite me. He was marking me, an unknown. I should have been shadowing him. It was an object lesson on how a top player approached his duties on the pitch and I never forgot it. As it happened, Serge didn't stop me when I scored a try in our 12–8 defeat of France. There again, where was I when he scored his?

After Sydney, I returned to make my debut for the Barbarians and flew back to the Far East to join the Irish Wolfhounds in the Hong Kong Sevens. My team-mates included Hugo O'Neil, Willie Anderson, Brendan Mullin and Michael Kiernan. Any trip with the Irish is likely to be fun-filled, and since I had been in the Welsh team who had beaten Ireland at Dublin a few months earlier there was plenty of added banter. Unfortunately, in the second match I pulled a hamstring, which was due to doing more socializing than training, and I was out of the competition.

It was also the end of my chances of playing for the British Lions v. The Rest at Cardiff on my return and for the Five Nations v. The Overseas at Twickenham three days later. It was a heavy price to pay for a fun trip to Hong Kong. I was sorry not to get my British Lions cap. I would have been devastated had I known that I was not going to be around when the next chance came.

The injury cleared up in time for me to accompany Wales on their tour of Fiji, Tonga and Western Samoa. There were times in the next two months when I wished it hadn't. It was my first tour and the hardest I've ever been on in terms of the physical nature of the rugby and the difficulty of the conditions. I'm not surprised at the progress all three countries have since made in both codes.

The demands of playing in the south Pacific brought my hamstring problem back and it was six weeks before I was able to resume in the Neath team. Since I had also missed a large chunk at the end of the previous season, I was not exactly the most popular player in Neath. But the lay-off seemed to have done me good. In my first comeback game I scored a try against South Wales Police, and in my next, against the reigning champions Pontypool, I scored two tries and two drop-goals. One writer called it 'one of the best individual performances turned in at club level in the past ten years'.

It was the game against Bath that gave us the most satisfaction and put me back in everyone's good books. We had taken Bath's ground record the previous season, but since then they had won the John Player Cup for the third consecutive year and had every reason to claim to be England's top team. They came to the Gnoll determined to get revenge and, not unnaturally, the press billed it as the game to decide the unofficial title of best team in Britain.

We didn't leave much doubt as to who deserved that honour. Neath beat them 26–9 and I was variously and embarrassingly described as a 'genius', a 'destroyer' and a 'showman' in the London newspapers. John Billot of the *Western Mail* called it 'perhaps the finest game of his sensational career'. All I know is that it was a pleasure to play in that match. One of my proudest memories was to catch their flying winger Tony Swift with a touchline tackle. I dropped a goal in the second half and had a chance to drop another a little later. But as I shaped for a drop-goal I suddenly decided to run around the blind side. Although I was too busy to count at the time, the television showed that I went past five defenders before scoring. The try was shown over and over again on the box.

People were still coming to terms with my size. One reporter wrote after the Bath game: 'Even after one full international season, Davies still looks like a schoolboy who has been promoted to senior rugby. You worry for him . . . but the memory most will have carried away was the subtle mastery of the Neath stand-off.'

There was nothing Neath or I could do wrong at that time. I scored a try after 42 seconds against Coventry and dropped three goals against Llanelli and hit the post with another. *The Times* printed a profile on me entitled: 'A God to Rouse the Valleys'. Jacques Fouroux, the French coach, christened me 'the Diego Maradona of world rugby'.

This may seem an excessive amount of trumpet blowing, but I do it only to emphasize how well everything was going for me at that time and how stupid I was to threaten it all by shooting my mouth off. I've always had a habit of talking too much both on and off the field. If I thought something, I'd say it. I try to be a little more careful these days, but I am still not one for keeping my opinions to myself.

My blunder at that time would seem nothing now, but I paid a heavy penalty. I had been warned by friends to keep my views about professionalism to myself but, ever the cheeky one, I had firm views on the subject. I had an interview with a journalist called Peter Bills, who was writing a lengthy article about me in a new magazine called *Sportsweek*. In the course of a very long chat over lunch and a few glasses of wine, I talked as naturally as I always do. It was typical of my immaturity at the time, and it was only when I saw my words splashed over page after page that I realized what a fool I'd been. It wasn't even as if I was getting paid for it.

As well as going on at great length about the shortcomings of rugby union, and Welsh rugby union in particular, I went on to say that if someone came along with £100,000 plus a car and a house I could be persuaded to turn to rugby league. In fact, said the article, it was 99 per cent certain that was where I would eventually end up.

It was rugby's equivalent of a suicide note and, of course, the rest of the media were on to it in a flash. Not surprisingly, the WRU announced an immediate investigation into whether I had professionalized myself by announcing my availability to rugby league clubs. In those days, you couldn't mention the word league without risking a ban. Neither were they happy about my criticism of them. Not being as eloquent as Will Carling, the expression 'old farts' didn't come to mind, but I was eight years ahead of Will in giving them a bit of my mind. In the event, I didn't get away with it easily.

I had to do a fair amount of grovelling, writing letters of apology and appearing before them in person to plead forgiveness for my unguarded statements that 'had been taken out of context and manipulated for sensationalism'. Ironically, the *Sportsweek* magazine in which the offending words appeared closed down a few weeks later. I did feel I was likely to follow it into oblivion.

It was just as well that they regarded me as an important member of the side and one they didn't want to lose with the Five Nations coming up and the World Cup in Australia following at the end of the season. Had I been more expendable, I fear I would have got the chop. As it was, they accepted my explanation and decided to take no further action apart from refuting my suggestion that top Welsh players were being poorly treated and that the administrators were out of touch.

But there were many, Brian Thomas among them, who felt that I had been secretly punished. The theory in several quarters was that I had been about to be appointed captain of Wales but that the article had changed people's minds. If that was true, it wasn't the only damage my words inflicted on me. They were about to cost me my place at Neath.

Before that split occurred, an even more serious gap had appeared in my life. All my gallivanting about the world in 1986, and my pre-occupation with rugby when I was home, led to strains in my relationship with Karen. Everything had been marvellous at first despite the fact that two days before the wedding our house deal fell through. Karen's parents offered to let us live with them and that turned out to be a blessing because we saw a lot more of her father in the final months of his life than we would have done. We eventually bought a house nearby with a lovely view down the valley and everything was fine until rugby took over more and more of my life. Being captain of Neath was a great honour but it also brought with it responsibilities to attend social and official functions in the town. In January 1987, we separated. Within two weeks we were back together, but less than a month later it was obvious that things weren't working out so we split up again. This time it was serious. We put our house up for sale and I moved into a flat in Neath.

This was happening while the *Sportsweek* episode was going on, which is more evidence that although everything was marvellous on the pitch I was being totally out of order off it. Living in Neath saved me a lot of travelling, but it wasn't long before the 'joys' of bachelor life began to pall. I was soon spending more time at my mother's and Ken's home in Trimsaran.

Any hopes I had that the Five Nations would make up for my lack of happiness at that time didn't last long. We won only one match, 19–12 against England at Cardiff, and although the other games were fairly close and a couple could have gone either way, we didn't get the chemistry right. It certainly did not provide a boost to our morale for the forthcoming World Cup.

During this time, the bonds that tied me to Neath were being slowly loosened. It was the last thing I wanted and yet I seemed powerless to stop it. Brian had been highly vocal in pressing my claims to be Wales's captain. 'He dictates every game, deciding exactly what the game is going to do. He is a leader in every sense. It is almost like playing chess. He is three moves ahead of the game. If people can't see that, they must be blind,' he told the press.

But what I had said in that fateful article began to get to him. There had been rumours the previous season that Cardiff were interested in me, but I assured him I wanted to stay with Neath. Now I had foolishly put the subject back on the agenda, and he took my marriage problems as a further sign that I was restless. He is such a thorough manager that he couldn't stand having doubts about the future make-up of the team. If I was going, he wanted to start re-organizing the team immediately. I told him that I had no thoughts of leaving. He and Neath were everything to me.

Unfortunately, that didn't satisfy him. He wanted to know at that precise time that I was sure to be at Neath the following season. There were no contracts in those days. Players were free to come or go more or less as they pleased. But he wanted a personal undertaking, there and then, that I would stay. It became an ultimatum. I can honestly say that I had no intention of going north at that time. I had received no offer since the one from Leeds, and what I told them still applied: I wanted to spend more time in union. I was happy at Neath and had no desire to leave.

But supposing I gave Brian a personal commitment and six months later received an irresistible offer from a league club that might never be repeated? No rugby union player in the world was required to tie himself to one club for a specified time. Why should I?

All I wanted to do was to go to the World Cup and come home and play for Neath. Beyond that I couldn't see. There was no need for this showdown. But, obviously, the more I resisted giving the commitment he wanted, the more Brian was convinced I had something lined up.

At the end of April, Neath shocked me and the rest of the rugby world by announcing: 'Because he has failed to make his future intentions clear, Jonathan Davies can no longer be considered as part of the progression plan of Neath RFC. Whatever code, country or club he will be involved with in future Neath RFC wishes him the best of luck.' Stuart Evans was named as captain – and he went north before I did.

It was two years before I accepted the Widnes offer. I swear that I would have remained at Neath for that period of time. People still seem to think that I wouldn't give the undertaking because I wanted to join Llanelli. That is not true. Llanelli turned me down when I was a boy while Neath gave me a chance. I'll never forget that, and I curse the day I agreed to that article. It stopped me repaying my debt to the club and to Brian.

Not long after that I left with the Welsh squad for the World Cup in Australia. I didn't have a wife, or a club to come back home to.

I wish I could report that I consoled myself by playing a blinder in Australia. I thought Robert Jones, John Devereux and Paul Moriarty were our stars. We finished third, which was highly creditable, but I was a little disappointed with my contribution. The trouble with success is that your own expectations, and those of other people, tend to rise too sharply for you to keep up with. But there were high spots. When Moriarty was injured, I was made captain against Canada and we scored eight tries against them in the second half. There was a call for me to be retained as captain, but the selectors managed to resist it.

Having also beaten Ireland and Tonga in our group we went on to beat England in the quarter-finals but were then smashed 49–6 by New Zealand in the semis. We gained some consolation by beating Australia 22–21 in the third-place play-off, but since they had only 14 men for most of the game it was rated a dubious distinction.

I have no doubt that my break with Karen affected my game. That, plus the parting from Neath, ate into my self-confidence just enough to take the edge off. I've always tried not to take problems on to the pitch, but my game depends very much on my spirits being high. It was, to a lesser extent, similar to my experience when I joined Cardiff.

It was no better when I returned. I had been making frequent calls home to Karen during the tournament, daring to hope that things might return to normal when I returned home. But when the Welsh squad got back after a 27-hour journey she was the only wife not waiting to greet us. In fact, she was just about to leave for a holiday in Miami. It was a classic piece of role reversal. She was bound for an exotic destination and I was the one feeling abandoned at home.

There was also the small matter of finding a club to play for. I was hoping to have some time to sort out my personal life, but no sooner was I back than the media speculation began. At first everyone was certain that I was going to Llanelli – some said Karen wouldn't come back to me if I didn't go there – then it was Swansea, and then Cardiff. The rumours then said I was conducting an auction and would join the highest bidder.

I was still upset at leaving Neath and would have been delighted to go back to the Gnoll if they'd have me. But they had made their decision and there was only one other club I was interested in: Llanelli.

So, six years after I had left Stradey as a glum 17-year-old reject, I walked back in to sign on for the club of my boyhood dreams. 'I am coming to run, not to kick,' I informed them.

Now that I was settled, I was eagerly looking forward to the new season and it was great joining my brother-in-law Phil Davies at my first training session. Phil and I had made our Welsh debuts together. In fact, it was after we both celebrated a Welsh victory too well that Phil met my sister. Caroline had come to collect me, and Phil had to carry me into the car and carry me out when we got home. Seven months later they were married. And to complete the family reunions, Karen and I got together again. We were back where we started: with Karen's mother Vireen in Cefneithin.

Then I did one of those stupid things for which I was becoming famous. I agreed to play in the Lord's Taverners Sevens. Unfortunately, I neglected to ask Llanelli's permission to play in what I saw as a chance to develop some pre-season sharpness and help a good cause.

The inevitable happened. I injured my knee and put myself out for ten weeks. A lot of supporters had bought season tickets on the strength of my return to Stradey, and they weren't happy, to say the least. It brought another load of critical publicity. I even received a rebuke from my mentor Phil Bennett which hurt.

I learned a couple of painful lessons from that escapade. The first was to start learning to say the word 'no' when people requested me to play in charity games, and the second was to make sure I was covered for injury. After I hurt my knee, which just locked solid, I was carried off and dumped on the dressing-room table. People popped in to see if I was able to get back on the field, but when it was obvious that my rugby was over for a while I was totally ignored. One minute I was the shining light, the next I was a useless lump of meat.

There I was, my knee so locked I couldn't put my trousers on, frantically trying to work out how I was going to get home to Wales, when Cliff Morgan walked in to see how I was. He saw my distress at suffering such a bad injury and called a taxi. He told the driver to take me to Cefneithin and send the bill to the Lord's Taverners. The fare was £525.

My debut finally came three months later and I promptly pulled a hamstring. But even when I did get into the team I appeared to disappoint people for not doing enough individually. The fact that I was concentrating on adjusting to a new style of play and not just trying to be flashy on my own account didn't occur to them. It was neither the first nor the last time I met that problem. To earn a name for spectacular play and jinking runs is to create an appetite you cannot always satisfy. The truth is that I am a fervent team player. I like to control matters, but everything I do in a match is directed towards helping the team win.

At Neath, where we had highly mobile forwards, I took the responsibility to make the breaks and set things up. People called me selfish, but we didn't score 113 tries in 25 games through selfishness.

At Llanelli, where there was also a great pack, they had some super backs, not least my friend and Welsh colleague Ieuan Evans. I saw it as my duty to make sure players like him saw plenty of the ball. So instead of making breaks I made sure I fed the centres with quick ball. I might not have looked like a star, but the team only lost two games.

In the meantime, while I was injured, Wales had played an international against American Eagles and won 46–0. Playing at outside half was Bleddyn Bowen, an excellent player with a different style to mine. The opinion was voiced that perhaps Wales should have a more orthodox outside half like Bleddyn instead of a box of tricks like me. What could I make of that? Too flamboyant for Wales, not flamboyant enough for Llanelli.

My mind, however, was on the far more pleasant subject of Karen. Our reconciliation was celebrated by her becoming pregnant. We had a scare when she crashed the car, but she was unhurt. Two days later I had a crash from which I emerged unhurt but disgraced. I had been to the funeral of the famous little Welsh referee, Gwyn Walters. Everybody was there and we had the customary drink or two. I should have taken a taxi or begged a lift, but I climbed into the car and felt so hungry I stopped for an Indian take-away.

Some reports said I was eating an onion bhaji as I was going along, but this was not true. Suddenly the car skidded when I came to the outskirts of Felinfoel, shot across the road and demolished a lamp-post. I wasn't hurt, but the police soon arrived and I failed the breathalyser test. I discovered later that someone tried to buy the lamp-post as a souvenir.

I couldn't believe I could get into so much trouble in the space of 12 months. There was a time, they say, when Wales's outside half could get away with murder. That was probably before the breathalyser. I was given a two-year ban. It seemed they wanted to make an example of me. I didn't complain. I deserved everything I got.

Later that week, I was captain of the Probables in the final Welsh trial. The Possibles won 7–3.

CHAPTER 12

From Triple Crown to *Titanic*

Ironically, 1988 was not only the year in which Jonathan was pushed despairingly towards the waiting arms of rugby league; it also marked some of his greatest achievements in union. This most significant period in his life, however, found an unpleasant way of introducing itself.

Still reeling from the blows of 1987, Jonathan was fighting hard to regain his place in the Welsh team when he was hit by a sucker punch that I feel the Daily Mirror *had been saving up until the moment of maximum embarrassment; i.e. the start of the Five Nations Championship in January.*

While Jonathan had been separated from Karen many months previously, he took out a young lady from Port Talbot. He enjoyed her company and was even introduced to her parents. But they never lived together and the brief encounter came to an end when Jonathan decided to dedicate himself to getting back with Karen. When he and Karen were eventually reunited he confessed to the dalliance and that was that, or so they thought.

The girl decided to complain to the Daily Mirror, *and it looked like they waited patiently until the eve of the international season before launching a front-page story under a large headline denouncing him as a 'Rugby Rat'. The embarrassment doesn't need to be described, especially to a man living under his mother-in-law's roof. Fortunately, Vireen was already aware of the matter, as was everyone else in the family. Whereas Jonathan has been exceedingly unlucky in losing the main male influences in his life, he has been compensated by the strength of the women around him. His mother and sister, Karen and her mother, have been pillars of steadiness whenever his equilibrium has been threatened by both the good and the bad times.*

It helped that the story hardly qualified as a scandal. He was separated from Karen at the time, and he didn't leave the girl at the altar or even on the steps of a maternity home. Indeed, the extent of her complaint was that he sought and secured a reconciliation with his wife.

On the back pages, meanwhile, the debate raged about whether he should be chosen for Wales. Playing for Llanelli against London Welsh on Boxing Day, Jonathan scored 24 points, including two tries, while orchestrating a 44–13 victory. Two days later he played for the Barbarians in their traditional match at Leicester. In an excellent match, Leicester won 48–30, but not before Jonathan scored a 45-yard drop-goal and produced the try of the match when he weaved through most of the Leicester team to seal a performance that, according to one critic, 'totally eclipsed everyone else in sight'.

But it was Les Cusworth, Leicester's veteran outside half and inspiration of his team's victory, who was acclaimed the hero at the after-match dinner. One speaker said he hoped Cusworth would be selected for England in the forthcoming match against Wales. 'I hope so, too,' shouted out Jonathan in what was an unmistakably brash declaration that he would be happy to take on Cusworth at Twickenham.

It was a welcome display of the old cockiness, especially as Jonathan's place in that confrontation was by no means certain.

There is nothing new about Welsh arguments over who should play at outside half. It happens every year. No matter who is in possession of the No. 10 shirt, the claims of some young hot-shot from another valley are invariably being advanced. It is all part of the pressure, and too much had happened to tarnish his image for him to feel confident.

Luckily, he had some big names on his side. So many former Welsh heroes become writers and commentators they form a Mount Olympus of opinion. Barry John and Phil Bennett were firmly on his side. Gareth Davies wrote in the Sunday Express: 'He is now ready to accept the responsibility of leading Wales to greater honours.' John Taylor, the former Wales and British Lions wing-forward, said: 'Since his return from injury, he has trans-formed Llanelli from an unhappy shambles into a team of poise and purpose. Talk of leaving him out of the national team is nonsense.'

When the team to meet England was announced, Jonathan was at outside half but was not given the captaincy. The selectors produced a shock by dropping Paul Thorburn, the finest goal-kicker in Europe at the time, and replacing him with Anthony Clement, the young Swansea outside half who was one of Jonathan's rivals for the No. 10 shirt. With both centres, Bleddyn Bowen and Mark Ring, also accomplished at the outside-half position, Jonathan felt that they were making a point.

His response was electric. Wales beat England, and Les Cusworth, 11–3. Bleddyn Bowen, who had been made captain, commented: 'This was one of Jonathan's most influential games for Wales. He had a marvellous match and showed true brilliance.'

The following match, against Scotland at the Arms Park, brought him even greater praise. He scored a try that is still shown as a prime example of solo initiative, and dropped two goals in the last eight minutes to help Wales win a close match 25–20.

One of the critics he won over was former Welsh captain Mervyn Davies, who told a reporter: 'People have been comparing him to the greats but I couldn't see it. But against Scotland he took the game by the scruff of the neck. He was in charge and it was a wonderful spectacle.' Barry John himself agreed: 'Jonathan is now the team's inspiration and in his present mood the Triple Crown and the Grand Slam are there for the taking.'

The Triple Crown was secured in Dublin thanks to a late penalty by the recalled Paul Thorburn. But the Grand Slam was not to be. France won 10–9 at Cardiff and so shared the championship. At least Wales, who were given little hope, had produced winning rugby in a style reminiscent of the glorious Seventies. And for Jonathan came the added reward of the Whitbread Rugby World Player of the Year title. From suspect starter to the world's best in three matches is quite a leap forward.

But the bright international prospects of Wales and Jonathan, alas, were doomed not to last long. They began to disintegrate after a disastrous tour of New Zealand that summer and they haven't regained those heights since. A sad chapter of misadventure and mismanagement drove Wales into the doldrums and Jonathan into another country and another code.

That season, however, had one more gripping performance to witness before the rot set in. Llanelli were steaming their way towards the Welsh Cup Final, and steamrollering from the opposite direction to meet them were Neath, who had made an excellent recovery following the loss of Jonathan and were now clear-cut favourites to win the Cup.

Anyone who saw the final as anything but a battle of tactical wits between Jonathan and his former mentor Brian Thomas had no feeling for high drama.

After more than 15 years of playing rugby in places where they take it very seriously, I suppose I know as much as anyone about the bitterness of local rivalry. In the West Wales leagues, between the 'Turks' of Llanelli and the Swansea 'Jacks', between Wales and England, between Widnes and St Helens, between Warrington and Widnes, Canterbury Bankstone and Western Suburbs. I've spent a career getting bruised in feuds that had nothing to do with me. I've taken it all in good part and enjoyed the extra intensity it has brought to matches.

But I've never felt as personally intimidated as I was before the Schweppes Welsh Cup Final at the National Stadium, Cardiff, in May 1988. The card arrived on the morning of the match. I saw the postmark and thought how nice it was that someone from Neath should send me good wishes.

Then I opened it and saw my photograph on the front. There was a noose drawn around my neck and the letters RIP written beneath. There was no message, just the signatures of the entire Neath team. Perhaps it was a joke, but jokes don't make your stomach turn over and your skin shiver.

It so happens that Neath have a reputation for an original line in horseplay. I know because I joined in some myself. I have also been on the receiving end. I once fell asleep on the team coach on the way back from a match and woke up feeling a little damp and smelling funny. They had used me as a urinal. I was able to laugh at that because it was our bit of fun and being captain did entitle me to certain privileges. And I was able to get my own back in various ways I needn't go into. A hideous variety of practical jokes are a large part of the enjoyment of playing rugby, and Neath indulge more heartily than most.

But I didn't find the noose at all funny and I don't think it was meant to be. Rivalry between teams is one thing, but when a whole

team selects one opponent for their target I don't find it acceptable, and I lost respect for certain members of the Neath club.

When I got to the ground, I showed the card to the rest of the
Llanelli team and they didn't think it was funny either. They urged
me to show it to someone in the press. I just tore it up and thought
to myself – right, you bastards, there's no way you're going to win
this game.

I'd played alongside most of those Neath players for four
seasons. I worked hard, played some good rugby and shared a
lot of success with them. When I left, which was not of my own
choosing, they were at the top. I was sincere when I wished them
all the best. I had to admit they'd done well without me. Not that I
expected them to collapse the moment I left, but it does take time
to replace a key player and change your style to suit the newcomer.

I certainly had to change my style to suit Llanelli's policy of
bringing their back division into action as often as possible, and
when the final against Neath loomed we had to think very hard
about the best way to tackle them. Their strength was still based
on a strong and mobile pack, and we had had a taste of that power
when they beat us 57–9 at the Gnoll. We didn't have a full team
out, but it was still a nasty reminder of how good they were.

Our coach, Gareth Jenkins, was convinced that our best hope
lay in surprising Neath by preparing our forwards both physically
and organizationally to take Neath on up front. I was to change
my approach accordingly and Neath were to face a type of
opposition they didn't expect.

Like all the pundits, Brian Thomas and Ron Waldron expected
that the game would be a straight conflict between different styles
– their power and pace in the pack against the speed and skill of
our backs. They planned accordingly, and while we announced
our team well in advance, Brian kept his formation a secret until
an hour before the kick-off.

Then he dropped a bombshell by leaving out their giant No. 8
Mark Jones in order to play three flankers in the back row and
thereby quicken their attack on me. If they could nail me regularly,
it would not only give them great pleasure but cut off the supply to
the Llanelli threequarters.

But we had no intention of playing to what was regarded as our
strength. We were going to play almost exclusively to our

forwards, who proceeded to have the game of their lives. Phil May and Phil Davies were brilliant, and our front five won a share of possession that was way beyond expectations. At scrum-half Jonathan Griffiths took all the right options, and when David Pickering, the fast Neath flanker deputed to contain me, came looking for me I just kicked for position.

It was a tremendous day. The attendance of 57,000 was a world record for a club match and every time I touched the ball the Neath fans booed and whistled as if I was the villain in a pantomime. What with that, and the memory of the card, I had all the incentive I needed.

Anyone watching Llanelli for the first time wouldn't have thought we had any backs, because every time I got the ball I kicked it. Negative? No, very positive. We had the advantage of a stiffish breeze in the first half and I was getting 60 or 70 yards on my touch kicks, which all bounced just right. To keep driving back down the field, to avoid mistakes and to put them under continual pressure; those were our aims and they worked a treat, especially as the absence of Mark Jones helped us win plenty of extra line-outs.

The Neath forwards became so annoyed they began giving away penalties. I scored four penalties, each one to a chorus of boos and jeers. I got hammered a couple of times in late tackles, but I expected that. The important thing was that we won 28–13, and even Neath had to acknowledge that we walked away with it. Then I was named Man of the Match by the biggest margin ever recorded. I can't remember being happier.

The Cup marked the end of a remarkable four months for me. What with the *Daily Mirror*'s nasty story and my drink-driving case, I'd had a lousy start to the year, but in no time at all I was back on top of the world. It was like a dream, and certainly not one I could have anticipated, even though I was chosen to play outside half in the first match against England. I knew there was a faction in the WRU who would be happy to see me replaced or at least moved to full-back. As it was, they put in Anthony Clement in place of Paul Thorburn. Everyone seemed thunderstruck by this. Paul's brilliant kicking was mainly responsible for Wales gaining third place in the World Cup. Now he was to be thrown out to make room for a 20-year-old who not only had never played a full game for Wales, he'd never played full-back at all.

▲ 21. Scoring for Widnes in our victory over Leeds in the John Player Trophy final of 1992.

◀ 22. Homecoming: John Devereux and I celebrate Widnes winning the 1990 Charity Shield against Wigan – our first game on Welsh soil since going north.

23. Welsh National Anthem – as sung by the exiles. The Welsh rugby league team, re-established in 1991, line up for their first match against Papua New Guinea.

24. With the World Club Championship Trophy after Widnes had beaten Canberra Raiders at Old Trafford in 1989. My other trophy was a Raiders shirt.

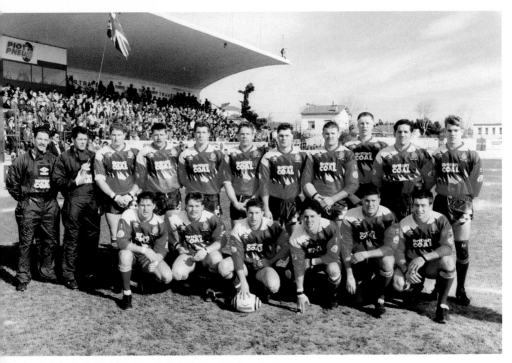

25. Captain of Great Britain against France in Perpignan in 1992.

26. In action for Canterbury-Bankstone in the Australian Rugby League 1993.

27. I score the try that helped Great Britain beat Australia at Wembley in October 1994.

28. Great Britain teammates Garry Connolly (3) and Jason Robinson help me celebrate the winning try.

Rugby league's European Cup – in Welsh ∣ds for the first time for almost 60 years.

30. Scott Davies, Welsh mascot, gets a lift from the Welsh captain after the World Cup victory over Western Samoa in 1995.

31. My last game in rugby league – in the World Cup semi-final against England at Old Trafford in 1995.

32. Captain of the Wales rugby league team.

33. Crunched by a tackle by Great Britain colleague Daryl Powell in Australia. He wa playing for the Gold Coast and I was playin for Canterbury.

34. Grappling with a python at Townsville Zoo, north Queensland.

35. A kiss from Grace after Wales beat Western Samoa in the World Cup 1995.

6. I avoid a flying tackle from Jason Martin to score a match-winning try for Canterbury against
orths.

7. Me and the Sydney Opera House.

38. At the Palace to receive the MBE.

It was not so much the decision as the way it was announced that sticks in the memory. Paul had done wonders for Wales and deserved a quiet warning. With extraordinary insensitivity for the feelings of players, he didn't know until the team was read out in the dressing-room. The look of devastation on his face told what a shock it was.

The experience didn't cheer me, but it focused my mind on the threat to my own place in the team and it did wonders for my motivation. In the event Anthony had an excellent game, but we did miss Paul's boot. We didn't once put the ball through the posts. It is very odd that just over a year later I was in rugby league and sticking the ball over with monotonous regularity. In union I played 27 times for Wales and hardly kicked a goal. Admittedly, Thorburn was in the side most of the time, but it still seems odd that I became a successful kicker overnight when I went north.

Beating England at Twickenham was a terrific result for a side few people believed in. It was a very satisfying match for me. Some said it was the best international I had played, but I was disappointed I didn't score a try. I had a part in both the great movements that led to two Welsh tries, but although I broke away in the first half I was tackled a couple of yards from the line by Jon Webb, the England full-back. I am told that a voice in the press box shouted, 'He is not as quick as he was.' I think I may have answered that allegation since, but the remark proves that some people prefer to be negative rather than positive. That man preferred to think that Webb caught me because I was slow. Let me put the record straight: it was a great tackle. It was the quickness of Webb's legs that saved England, not the slowness of mine.

I proved that later on when I went on a wide loop left of the England defence, shaking off Mickey Skinner who'd already given me one thump, and setting off a passing chain that led to Adrian Hadley scoring a try.

I'd hurt my ankle when Webb tackled me and it swelled up like a balloon later. Fortunately, it improved for the following match against Scotland at Cardiff. That turned out to be a magnificent game and one of the most personally rewarding I've ever played in. Alan Tait, who was to become a team-mate at Widnes, played in the centre for Scotland that day and never ceased to remind me how close they came to beating us. They were a super side, but I had the good fortune to be given the chance to score a try I still think about.

My game is based on instinct, but I always have trouble convincing people of how much my game is governed by it. We were 7–0 down and desperately trying to get into the game when I had a flash of instinct that was wholly responsible for a try that we badly needed. It is one of my favourite tries, because it proves one of my theories that very often bad ball can be better for the adventurous player.

Every stand-off loves the ball that comes whizzing into his arms as he comes running on to it. But even as he takes it, the opposition are moving into position to cut down his options. So, good ball for you is red alert for them. But a poor pass, one you have to pull off your toes or pluck out of the air, creates that moment of doubt about your next move not only in your mind but in your opponents'. And a moment of doubt in their mind is the best ally you can have.

The try I scored against Scotland was unusual enough to get it played over and over again on television, and many people have asked me why I did what I did. The answer, which I am never sure they understand, is that the pass was so bad it confused Scotland more than it confused me.

What happened was that we had a scrum about 18 yards from the line and just a few yards in from the right touchline. We won the scrum but the ball squirted out unkindly for Robert Jones. He had to move sideways and backwards to reach the ball and, with the Scottish scrum-half Roy Laidlaw almost on him, he flicked the ball high in my direction. Since he had his back to me at the time, it was a great piece of work.

His pass, however, presented me with the outside half's worst scenario: standing flat-footed, waiting for a dropping ball while the killer wing-forward Finlay Calder was coming at me from one direction and their outside half Andrew Ker from another. Had Robert's pass been straight and true I would have had a problem. Finlay would have been coming at me like a bull, because he was one of the quickest-breaking wing-forwards in the game, and he would have been sizing me up, deciding what my move was going to be and flinging himself to stop me. But because the ball had yet to drop into my arms he was in doubt about what to do. Because it was a bad ball there was an option he didn't consider. I didn't consider it either. I just did it.

I caught the ball and ran back the way it had come, side-stepping Finlay and kicking the ball low between him and the scrum which was starting to break up. There was a channel barely a yard wide stretching between me and the line and the ball went through it like a bullet with me in pursuit.

Derek White, Scotland's big No. 8, was the only one who could turn and chase after the ball. He had a few yards' start, but I was already moving at full pace and I went past him on the line to pounce on the ball and score. I hope Derek realized I was joking afterwards when I said that if I couldn't beat someone as slow as him I would pack the game in.

The whole movement, from catching the ball to scoring, was pure instinct. I hardly had time to think. I just obeyed the orders of my brain. Had I paused for a split second, either Finlay would have had me or the gap would have disappeared. That's what I mean about a bad ball being a good one. Scotland were thrown by it more than I was. It still took two drop-goals in the last eight minutes to clinch our victory, but that try was decisive and convinced me, if ever I needed convincing, that the instinctive act is sport's deadliest weapon.

We clinched the Triple Crown in Dublin with an action that was the exact opposite of instinctive. There is nothing more calculated than a kick at goal. When it is to win the Triple Crown, the accompanying pressure can't be imagined. The score was 9–9 with less than a minute left when we were awarded a penalty. It was not an easy kick: on the left, about 35 yards out, and a swirling wind to contend with. After all the flair, all the flowing rugby that had brought us that far, everything now depended on one cold and deliberate kick. If it goes over we make history; if it doesn't we *are* history. Paul had been uncaringly tossed aside for our first match, and now everything depended on him.

He put it over high and true and we won Wales's only trophy of the Eighties. Had he failed it would have been with him for the rest of his life. I went on to take many vital kicks in league and I hated every one of them. Acting on impulse, no matter how audacious, doesn't impose pressure, but kicking is the most thankless job of all. The more you kick, the more they expect you to kick. I scored some great tries in league, but the pleasure was immediately ruined by one thought – now I've got to convert the bloody thing.

We didn't play well against Ireland because we allowed the pressure to build up into a fear of losing. The people who criticized us for not sparkling more tended to forget that it was a relentless struggle against a side that yielded nothing, and to win was a tribute to the team's effort and courage. We had won the Triple Crown the hard way, with two out of the three matches away from home.

But I couldn't deny to myself that we would have won more comfortably by sticking to our guns and spinning the ball. Instead, we froze and kicked away good possession. In my anxiety to get points on the board, I certainly tried too many drops at goal. I succeeded with an early one, which encouraged me to try a few more, but I should have concentrated more on getting the line going.

This lack of thought and awareness about ourselves as a team was typical at the time, and a serious flaw considering the amount of time Wales spent at squad sessions. I was happy to call the shots during the game but a general strategy that we all agreed with would have made a difference to our approach. Unfortunately the sessions were not used to foster teamwork and understanding. If we were not already fit at that stage of the season, we never would be, yet all we did was physical training.

To gather together the best players in South Wales just to do sprints and weights was a tremendous waste, especially when the forthcoming match was hardly talked about, let alone planned for. These views are not just with hindsight after a long time in the professional ranks. I thought them at the time and did myself no favours by expressing them.

The final match, against France at Cardiff, offered our first chance of the Grand Slam for ten years, and I decided to do my own planning. Everyone was expecting a fast handling game, which would have suited us. But, after being dry all week, it poured down on the day of the match and handling became a risky business. There was too much at stake for that and as a result neither team played to its potential.

I felt it was a day best suited to up-and-unders. Great as he was, Serge Blanco had a weakness in dealing with the ball dropping on him from a great height, especially if it was slippery and he had to turn. It was a tactic that frequently led us to within a few yards of the French line, but they kept us out, desperately at times. Had we scored then, I am sure we would have won, but the game sank into deadlock.

One of my surprises was called for and I felt cheeky enough to attempt to turn a drop-out from our 25 into a solo attack. I shaped to put the customary kick into the air for the forwards to fight over, but when the ball hit the ground I flicked it downfield with the outside of my foot. I hared after it and hacked it another 30 yards. I was up to the half-way line before a Frenchman came near the ball. I gave another whack and reached their 25 before someone caught me. The situation looked promising for a minute or two but they beat us back. Then my opposite number Lescarboura managed to score a try with three of us hanging on to him, and although Ieuan replied they won 10–9. We still shared the championship, but the Grand Slam had gone and Wales haven't so much as smelt it since.

When the whistle went, I happened to have the ball in my hand and thought I'd keep it as a souvenir. I was making my miserable way up the tunnel when I felt an arm on my shoulder. It was Daniel Dubroca, the French captain and hooker. He nodded at the ball. Then I remembered it was his last game for France, whom he had captained 25 times. He is the only man ever to captain a team to three consecutive Five Nations Championships. I held out the ball and he took it with a smiling 'Merci'. Had I known it was the end of my Five Nations career, I would have kept it myself.

Although even the thought would have been ridiculous at the time, it was also to be the end for many of that Wales set-up. Our reward for winning the Triple Crown was to be sent on the most disastrous expedition Welsh rugby had ever embarked upon. And it was so unnecessary.

Those of us who had played against New Zealand in the World Cup the previous year wondered from the outset why we were going there of all places. They'd murdered us 49–6 in the semi-finals at Brisbane. We felt that we had improved considerably as a team, but Bleddyn Bowen and I agreed it was a suicide mission.

And that was before we'd examined the itinerary. It had been slung together in a totally amateurish and ill-informed manner. What slim chances we had were killed before we started. Even the New Zealanders were horrified. Instead of starting with the easier matches to allow us to acclimatize and build up confidence for the first Test, we were flung in immediately against the toughest provincial teams.

We were already reeling when we met the full might of the All Blacks at Christchurch and were demolished 52–3. By the time we were due to play the second Test at Eden Park we were looking an even sorrier sight. Captain Bleddyn Bowen had been flown home injured and vice-captain Bob Norster then joined the lengthening list of wounded. I was made captain, and somebody said it was like being put in charge of the *Titanic*.

We did, however, stage a minor fight-back. I scored a late drop-goal that allowed us to beat Otago 15–13, and I scored a record 21 points, including two tries, when we beat Hawkes Bay 45–18. Then came the second Test and although the 54–9 scoreline looks gruesome we managed to pull some dignity out of the wreckage. We had two new caps in the team – Jonathan Griffiths, my scrum-half partner from Llanelli, and Kevin Moseley, the Pontypool second-row – and although morale was shaky we went out determined to give it all we had.

Wayne Shelford, the New Zealand skipper, said afterwards that if we had played all the games as we played in the first 20 minutes they would have had a hard time beating us. But the game just ran away from us. Grant Fox gave the best kicking display I'd ever seen. He scored goals from everywhere, and it was thanks to him the score looked so bad.

At least I came away with something. I ran almost the length of the pitch to score a consolation try and was amazed to get a standing ovation on my way back. I was more shocked when I was named Man of the Match and I still treasure the wrist watch that came with the title. But I was even prouder of the amount of tackling I did. I told the boys we had to tackle our hearts out and I thought I'd better lead the way.

To cap my collection of proud moments from that game was the presence of Ray Gravell, the redoubtable Llanelli, Wales and British Lions centre who could tackle a Cromwell tank. He remembers my father taking me to watch Llanelli when I was a toddler. He once presented the prizes at Trimsaran Primary when I was there. That's how he still saw me until that game. 'The boy had become a man,' he said.

Ray had become a popular broadcaster for BBC Wales and I couldn't have wished for a better source from which to receive the following compliment on my performance:

> There was no way Wales could win this match. There was no way they could avoid a massive defeat, they were so heavily out-gunned. But Jonathan led them out there to give every last ounce of effort and he was determined to lead by example. It was like Rorke's Drift, only with All Blacks instead of Zulus which is probably worse.
>
> He showed everything I admire in a sportsman. It is not often you get so much skill and bravery in one body. He proved he is world class that day. He was tackling men he had no business to tackle, the big back-row men Shelford, Jones and Whetton didn't frighten him at all.

After the match, I attended the usual press conference and tried to be realistic. Instead of complaining about our luck or the fact that Fox scored ten goals from all over the place, I tried to be honest and take a positive view of our problem. At least one reporter, Stephen Jones of the *Sunday Times*, appreciated it. He wrote:

> He had tackled the All Blacks and now he was ready to tackle the problems confronting Wales. He saw the defeats as a revelation and he knew what was needed to bring Welsh rugby up to that standard. He wanted to tell the Welsh Rugby Union's AGM all about it when they got home.
>
> It wasn't arrogance talking. It was a young man who had shared in a bitter, almost degrading, series of defeats yet was excited by the possibilities for improvement that had been opened up. There had been so little rational analysis in the Welsh party of what they were up against. They were being outclassed and out-thought and yet they just kept plodding along without reacting or responding. He was the only one prepared to face the facts, as unpalatable as they were.

The point is that he knows the game inside out. He has a magnificent tactical brain and is not afraid to use it. I talked with him a lot during the World Cup the previous year and was impressed then by his grasp of the game. I think he knew what was coming and yet he walked into that New Zealand tour with his head high – and that's how he walked out of it. He was so clearly the man to lead and inspire Wales.

My request to be allowed to address the WRU's AGM on the subject of being called the worst major touring team ever to visit there was treated with contempt. I didn't get a reply and I understand they were not happy at my impudence. But it wasn't only me. Bleddyn Bowen, the original captain, had returned early because of injury, but the vice-captain Bob Norster saw the tour through and he was very keen to prepare a report along with other senior players. He wanted the players' point of view put forward in the hope it might help frame a new policy. They might have thought I was a cheeky upstart, but Bob was one of the best and most respected players in the world. His offer fell on deaf ears, too.

Nor were the coaches, Tony Gray and Derek Quinnell, asked for their opinion. They sacked them instead. The best coaches the world has ever seen could not have stopped the All Blacks destroying us. Tony and Derek had seen us through to a rare Triple Crown a few months earlier, and now they were sacrificed because of a stupid decision made by someone else.

The Welsh squad that had brought us success that spring was fresh, talented, well balanced and full of confidence and potential. If we hadn't been sent on that senseless tour and had visited, instead, a less demanding country, we could have developed our style and worked on the understanding that had built up between the coaches, the captain Bleddyn Bowen and the players. We would have returned to face Western Samoa and Romania in very good shape and could have looked forward to the 1989 Five Nations with more genuine hope of success than any of our rivals. I, for one, would not have walked out had that been the scene.

But once they sacked the coaches, the new regime seemed intent on dismantling the memory of New Zealand by changing the squad. Adrian Hadley had already gone north – to be followed by me and Paul Moriarty and several others – as a direct result of the New Zealand aftermath. Bleddyn Bowen was treated appallingly. Richie Collins and Phil May were soon to disappear. It was no coincidence that Wales had its lowest ever representation when the 1989 British Lions were announced.

From joint European champions to a sad mess in the space of a couple of months – and no sign that the WRU even wondered why.

CHAPTER 13

Scapegoat Heads North

Not long after his rebuff by the WRU, Jonathan had a call from St Helens Rugby League Club asking if he was interested in a chat. He agreed to meet their chairman Joe Pickavance in Aberystwyth where Jonathan's employers at the time, Stirling Finance, have their head office. They talked in general terms about cash and contracts and agreed to meet at a later date.

On 19 July, Jonathan and his solicitor Malcolm Struel met Pickavance at his St Helens home where a formal offer was made. It was a good deal but Jonathan wanted more time to think.

Karen gave birth to Scott the following day so it was hardly a good time for careful consideration of a major upheaval. But Jonathan, in any case, was reluctant to leave union. Despite his frustration with Wales he realized that what he wanted most from rugby at that moment was not money. He desperately wanted to help to get Wales back on an even keel for the Five Nations; he wanted to go with the British Lions to Australia the following summer; and when the All Blacks visited Wales in October 1989 he wanted to be part of the Llanelli team who would be bidding to maintain their great record against the tourists. Perhaps more than anything, he also wanted to lead Wales in an attempt to avenge the humiliations suffered in New Zealand that summer.

These were ambitions exciting enough to keep any player occupied, and if he wanted to go north after that he would still be only just coming up to the age of 27. Besides, it was possible that the rules regarding union men earning money from peripheral activities might have been relaxed by then and that he could get his desired security without having to uproot the family.

He told St Helens of his decision and agreed they could contact him the following year to check if he was more receptive to an offer. He was sure he had done the right thing and faced the new season with rekindled enthusiasm. This was boosted when he helped Llanelli win the pre-season Snelling Sevens, scoring 46 points, and was declared Man of the Tournament.

The season, however, did not turn out to be a success. At domestic level he found it hard to pick up his game, probably because he was distracted by the prospect of two Welsh matches, against Western Samoa in November and Romania in December. In between he was selected for the Barbarians against Australia, who had been touring England and Scotland.

Wales beat Western Samoa, but not as convincingly as some were expecting. The Samoans were already on the way up and three years later were to beat Wales in the World Cup, but then they were regarded, with typical arrogance, as a team Wales should comfortably destroy. Accordingly, there were sweeping changes for the Romania game, including the dropping of Paul Thorburn in favour of Anthony Clement. It was the usual Welsh remedy of changing the faces instead of the formula. Apart from losing the advantage of Thorburn's deadly accurate goal-kicking, Jonathan found himself unhappy with the type of forwards they had chosen. He thought the game called for a bigger pack.

But he was upset most by a farcical incident in the week before the match. Mike Hall, then playing for Cambridge University and Bridgend, had been selected for the squad but replaced because, not surprisingly, he wanted to play in the Varsity match on the Tuesday. Mark Ring, the stylish Cardiff centre, was then dropped for turning up late for a training session. Bleddyn Bowen, the other centre in the squad, was the obvious choice to replace him but the selectors sent for Hall. Having decided he shouldn't play, because he chose to play for Cambridge, they then picked him instead of Bleddyn, who had captained Wales to the Triple Crown eight months earlier.

Jonathan found the whole business very unsettling and felt great sympathy for Bleddyn, who was shattered by the turn of events. Neither was he very happy that after their difficulty in overcoming Western Samoa no one had discussed with him what their approach should be against Romania. They must have had a reason for making changes but gave no explanation of what they had in mind.

He decided to use the same tactics that had made Wales the top team in Britain earlier that year. They would spread the ball wide, run and set up rucks and make the most of second-phase possession. It was not exactly original, and something a Welsh team playing at home should be able to perform. But although they ran and set up rucks, the bigger Romanian forwards were getting there in strength before the Welsh.

Had Jonathan scored with an early penalty which hit the post, had Wales scored from an exciting break he made that broke down five yards from the line through lack of support, had a Welsh forward not trodden on an opponent after they had been awarded a penalty in front of the posts . . . Wales could have had a comfortable early lead. But as the Arms Park echoed with the restlessness of a 17,000 crowd who gave the place none of its usual inspirational atmosphere, they stumbled from error to error.

Romania knew their best chance lay in spoiling and containing, and in their outside half, Gelu Ignat, they had a tremendous kicker who constantly drove Wales back with 60- and 70-yard boomers. They didn't pass the ball once and gradually ground their way to a 15–9 victory. They had given France a scare in Bucharest two weeks earlier, losing only 16–12, but this, said their coach, 'was the most important moment in our rugby history'.

Wherever the media and the Welsh fans gathered, the inquests bordered on the hysterical. Getting stuffed in New Zealand was one thing; being beaten by Romania at home was a disgrace. Jonathan knew he hadn't played well and hadn't reacted to the flow of the game. He should have changed the tactics by kicking more, playing like Romania in fact. But for a Welsh team to be reduced to kicking its way out of trouble against an emerging team would have been a failure in itself. He was more intent on trying to rekindle the fire of the expansive game that had won Wales the Triple Crown.

Within a few days it was generally agreed that it was all his fault. The following Tuesday he arrived for the usual Welsh squad training session and no one spoke to him apart from a curt greeting. Surely, with all the team and officials present, some sort of post-mortem should have been conducted. But they just trained and left. He was desperate to discuss what had gone wrong, perhaps get a consoling arm on his shoulder. Even a bollocking would have been more helpful than silence.

He thought that perhaps he should volunteer to give up the captaincy. He decided to ask the coach John Ryan for a meeting to chat about things. Three times he rang to speak to him and left messages. Eventually Ryan rang back but said he was busy. The one afternoon when it seemed they were both available, Ryan turned out to have a prior appointment with a journalist that he said he couldn't break. They never had the meeting and have never spoken about it since.

One man, far away from the scene, had been watching these events with a mixture of disbelief and delight. Doug Laughton, coach of Widnes, rugby league's leading team of the moment, had long been on Jonathan's trail. He knew of the abortive attempt St Helens had made to sign him six months earlier, but the willingness of the Welsh to make their captain the scapegoat after their Romanian defeat alerted him to a new situation.

Laughton already had the reputation as the league's most successful recruiting sergeant. He had been the man responsible for plucking Martin Offiah from the obscurity of the Rosslyn Park wing. He took Scottish centre Alan Tait and turned him into Britain's best full-back. While on a wet caravan holiday in Anglesey, Laughton watched a match, beamed from New Zealand, between a Welsh touring team and Wellington. He was so impressed with the Wellington No. 8, Emosi Koloto, that he decided to sign him as soon as possible. To sell a future in rugby league with Widnes over the telephone to a Tongan in New Zealand was an indication of his persuasiveness.

To offer a lucrative escape route to a besieged Welshman would seem child's play in comparison. He telephoned Jonathan at the height of the hue and cry just before Christmas. The response was less than encouraging, but Laughton sensed it was worth persevering.

He had his eye on Jonathan long before he had seen any of his other big signings; before he was coach, in fact. When the player made his debut for Wales against England in 1985, Laughton was in a pub watching the match on television. 'That boy can play,' he said, to no one in particular.

He maintained his watch on Jonathan's career and once recommended him to Wigan. Although he was coach at Widnes by then, they couldn't afford him and he felt very strongly that he would be great for the league game.

After Jonathan had played well in Llanelli's 38–15 victory over Swansea on the Monday after New Year's Day – Laughton had sent scout Eddie McDonnell down to watch him – Laughton asked the Widnes committee's permission to bid high for him. The fact that they were already the best team didn't mean that they shouldn't invest in a great prospect, he argued.

He rang Cefneithin again and couldn't have chosen a better time. It was late in the evening and Jonathan had just attended another Welsh squad session. The chill factor was even more noticeable. Far from wondering whether he would lose the captaincy, he now felt that even his place was in doubt. But still he resisted Laughton's argument that now was the time to move. The Widnes coach said he would come down the following day. It would be a wasted journey, warned Jonathan.

'Fair enough,' he said, 'but I want to be looking into your face when you tell me "no".'

Laughton set out for South Wales with Jim Mills, a Widnes committee man and a former playing partner of Doug in the Widnes and Great Britain teams. Jim was born in Cardiff and went north when he was still a teenager. He was well known in Wales not only as a good player but as a fearsome one with a record of being sent off over 20 times.

The pair had made many forays into Wales and were not a welcome sight. Understandably, representatives of rugby league clubs have been much loathed visitors to Wales for the best part of a century. Wales will now have to get used to predators from a different direction, from clubs like Harlequins, Richmond and Bath. But there was no doubting the enemy then. Doug was once ordered out of the Neath clubhouse. 'And take that big thug with you,' said the irate official, pointing at Jim. 'You tell him,' suggested Doug.

On this occasion they went straight to Jonathan's home, where the talk was not so much about money as about a player's pride, about having your career run by professionals and not bungling amateurs. He was still not convinced, but they left him plenty to mull over.

Laughton felt that their chances were no better than 50–50 when they left him. Remembers Laughton: 'Despite all his talk about running to league one day, deep down he didn't want to leave *home. And for all his supposed arrogance he wasn't sure he would succeed if he came. My hardest job was to convince him he could make it. He kept asking, "Are you sure?" The funny thing was that I didn't really need him. I had the best team already. I just knew it was in both our long-term interests if he joined there and then.'*

The Widnes men decided to stop for a drink. Jim immediately recognized the man who came to serve them. It was Norman Gale, the former Llanelli and Wales hooker, whose pub they had unwittingly chosen. Jim introduced Doug, and Norman eyed them suspiciously. 'What are you doing down here?' he asked. Jim made up a story about seeing Tony Clement, the Swansea player.

While they chatted, Jim casually asked him if he was still connected with the Llanelli club. 'Yes,' said Norman, 'I'm the chairman.'

Doug quietly choked on his beer. They were about to rob him of his best player.

When I returned to play union in Wales, it was like turning up late to a party; everybody was getting ready to leave. Not a week went past without news of another departure to an English club. Harlequins, Wasps, Saracens, Leeds, West Hartlepool, Richmond, Bristol . . . not even at the height of the defections to rugby league had there been anything to compare with this exodus.

There was a distinct difference, however. Never once did I hear the words like 'Judas' or 'traitor' that echoed after me and the others who went north in the late Eighties or early Nineties. None of those who left for the rich English union clubs was called a greedy little sod as I was. Yet there was probably more reason to question their motives than there was mine. Union was professional now so they could earn good wages at home. It wasn't a choice between earning a living from rugby or not earning a living at all, as it was in my day. They couldn't even say they were off to a new challenge, because in some cases they joined teams not as good as the ones they were leaving.

They took their decisions based on what they felt suited their career. They were going off to play the same game and had to forsake nothing. They could still play for Wales and come back whenever they felt like it. And no one questioned their right to do it. Neither do I.

But I can't help comparing their freedom to that available to me and a hundred or more like me over past decades. No one who hasn't taken the decision could know how desperately difficult it was to walk out for ever on the game and the country you loved. I was one of the fortunate few to be able to come back. My heart bleeds for those who never could.

It was like stepping into a flying saucer – you were going to a different world. It was worse than that. In the days after I signed for Widnes, it was like being dead and reading your obituaries in the newspapers. People were, talking gravely about how much I would be missed and what a tragedy it was. Llanelli players told how they were training with me the previous night and never realized I would go just like that.

I suppose I had died in a way. As far as Welsh rugby was concerned I had ceased to exist. I had become a non-person, to be talked about in the past tense. But suddenly there was a change in the way I was regarded. From being a load of rubbish after the Romanian game, I was being talked about in totally glowing terms. People say lovely things about you when you're gone; it is a shame they don't say them when you're still around. One kind word from the right people and I might not have gone.

I was grateful for the way Gerald Davies summed it up in *The Times* when he traced the reasons for my disillusion and ended: 'Those who have attempted to deny him his rightful place will now ponder long and hard at the gap his departure leaves.'

Stephen Jones in the *Sunday Times* was another whose generosity I appreciated. 'He has never been embraced as warmly by Wales as have the others in the great rolling dynasty of fly-halves . . . Yet for me Davies was unquestionably the greatest of all, the richest and the most complete talent. His single greatest failing is that he was born at the wrong time.'

Reading stuff like that made me wonder about my decision, but who knows what would have happened had I stayed? I might have been flung out like so many others, just another victim of the whims of the Welsh selectors.

There was much speculation about the real reason that drove me north. The money was usually listed as the major factor. The money was important, obviously. In the end, after ceaseless nagging, Doug asked me to name a figure that would force me to think seriously. I named what I considered a ridiculously high amount, partly in the hope it would get him off my back. 'You're on,' he said. I obviously didn't ask for enough!

But far deeper thoughts were bothering me. I'd seen at close hand how Paul Thorburn and Bleddyn Bowen had been treated; how when my scrum-half partner Robert Jones caught pneumonia they didn't even bother to phone to see how he was before they left him out. And there was the lesson of how I got into the Welsh team in the first place. Gareth Davies, after 21 caps, had been publicly insulted when the name A.N. Other appeared where his had been. As for my ambition to play for the British Lions, if I was to be dropped following the Romanian match I might never be selected. Unknown to me, Ian McGeechan, who had been appointed as Lions' coach, had already pencilled my name in as an early member of his squad.

I regarded myself as friendless and unappreciated, and the only soothing voices belonged to Doug Laughton and Jim Mills. The way they talked about their game impressed me. It appeared that nothing mattered except how good you were. I was desperately uncertain how I would fare in league, but if men of that quality were prepared to place their reputations on the line, why shouldn't I? They gave me more confidence in myself than I ever received from the WRU.

When I made my decision it was so quick it surprised even me. It's like being on the field. I suddenly decide to make a play and I'm gone before I know it. Many thought I had deliberately misled them by my constant denials that I was on the point of turning. But the four people most shocked by the move were Karen, my mother, my mother-in-law and me.

Karen had decided to resume her career once Scott was old enough to be left with her mother. She started back at the hospital 48 hours before I agreed with Widnes. My mother was convinced I wasn't going and, because I couldn't get through to her that morning, she was cheerfully telling reporters not to be silly when they rang up for a reaction. Vireen was similarly stunned. So was I.

Had I the remotest thought I might give in to Doug, I would not have left training that night without some sort of warning to my team-mates.

The media reaction to a world-record rugby league transfer was understandably fierce, and I was glad to leave on the Friday afternoon to drive up to Widnes – where I found the fuss was even worse. Widnes were playing in the John Player Special Trophy final at Bolton Wanderers' ground, Burnden Park, against Wigan the following day. I was due to appear at a press conference at the ground a few hours before, but I wouldn't get a chance to meet the players until after the game. Friday night was my chance to meet all the Widnes officials quietly.

I was booked into the Hillcrest, a hotel on the northern outskirts of Widnes, which was to be our home until we found a house. It was a bright and noisy place and presented nothing like the austere image I had of Widnes. We walked into the restaurant bar to be greeted by palm trees and smart cane furniture and a large brass-topped bar into which a piano had been built. The pianist was tinkling away as we drank our pints from tall thin glasses that would have been denounced as poncy back in Trimsaran.

Since all recruits to Widnes stayed there by courtesy of the owner Harold Nelson, the place did wonders in making new-comers feel at home. Pretty soon all the Widnes officials, including Doug Laughton, had turned up and a lively party built up. I kept having to leave the bar to take calls from the media, and on one of my visits to the phone I was surprised to see Steve Powell, who played in the centre with me at Neath. He looked as if he had been in a fight. His face was cut and his nose looked as if it had been ripped off and stuck back on again. He explained that he had come up to have a secret trial with Hull RLFC and they had put him into the 'A' team at Swinton that night. He'd found it hard going and felt that for the money they were offering it wasn't worth it. He was a tough player, and if he found it hard, how would I fare, I asked myself. It was a coincidence that he'd been booked into the same hotel, and I felt embarrassed as he went furtively off to bed in case someone else recognized him. I was being feted like a hero and he was having a lonely night after a miserable experience of playing rugby for a living.

I was soon to have an indication that my own future was nothing to feel secure about, because back in the bar Doug made a great show of presenting me with a Widnes shirt. It had No. 14 on the back – a not so subtle hint that a substitute's jersey was all I was entitled to at that time.

The car taking me to Burnden Park next day had barely rolled to a stop when the door was yanked open and I was posing for about fifty photographers. David Howes, the rugby league's press officer, then whisked me into the press conference which was packed with rugby reporters and feature writers up from London. I managed to get through it all without revealing my ignorance about league. I was interviewed on the pitch for BBC's *Grandstand* before being whisked off for lunch with Widnes's sponsors, ICI.

When I returned to Burnden Park I was introduced to the crowd amid a lot of cheering and chanting. If I had been a Widnes player listening to that lot from the dressing-room I would have been really pissed off. I was getting all the attention on what was their big day. I like to think that my arrival was not the reason they didn't play very well. In fact, Wigan beat them 12–6 and it was a lot less close than that. The Wigan players said afterwards that all the ballyhoo over my arrival worked in their favour because it made them all the more determined to remind people how well they could play the game.

When, at last, I met my new club-mates after the game I was given a very genuine welcome. And it wasn't just Widnes who seemed pleased to see me. Representatives of every league club were present and they all made a point of coming up to say how glad they were I had joined league. I must say they found a funny way of showing it over the next few months, but it made me realize how isolated they felt. They all saw my arrival as a chance for their game to get more recognition.

It was a while before all the fuss died down and before I became accustomed to all that was expected of me. Doug said he was going to give me my first taste of league the following Sunday, when they had a championship match against Salford at Naughton Park, but it would be only as a substitute. Over the next seven days I lost 12 pounds in weight directly from nervous tension. I could not afford to lose that much from a frame that northerners were already looking at with grave suspicion.

It was no surprise. References to my size had followed me all my life, so I could hardly expect to escape in a game so conscious of the physical side. I hadn't been in the Hillcrest for more than a few minutes when I was aware of people looking me up and down as if they couldn't believe that such a small package was worth such a lot of money. There were a few St Helens fans in the bar and they couldn't resist running their fingers down the bridge of my nose and warning me to take a long last look at it before its shape was altered.

I could take all that crap, but I was not prepared for the reaction of the Widnes physiotherapist when I presented myself to have my measurements taken for the club's medical records. Women physios are now commonplace in both codes of rugby, but I was a little shocked when I met Viv Gleeve, the young lady who looked after Widnes's aches and pains. It was bad enough to have to appear before her in a near-naked state, but to have her dissolve into peals of laughter was a bit unnerving.

Since any physical attributes I have are based mainly on my legs and hips, my upper body tended not to be impressive when I was in union. My arms, especially, were of the scrawny variety and not at all similar to any she would normally see in the Widnes dressing-room. She instructed me to gain a stone in a month. 'In the meantime,' she said, 'don't lie on the beach, you'll get sand kicked in your face.'

Then she examined me and found the scars of my knee operations, discovered I was slightly asthmatic and diagnosed, quite rightly, that I had a slight curvature of the spine. 'You're a walking disaster,' she told me, 'and that's before you've even walked on to the field.'

I had tried to get advice from previous union converts. David Watkins, now a good friend, was a particular comfort. Watkins was the reigning Welsh outside half and was even smaller than me when he joined Salford in a transition that created a similar sensation 22 years earlier. Watkins had been a brilliant success and his example and his words were very encouraging.

When David went north, he was signed on a Thursday and was thrown into his first game the very next day. He hadn't even looked at the rules. It was a terrifying experience, he told me. I waited 11 days, lost almost a stone through tension, and as I shivered on the substitutes bench waiting to go on I remember thinking that if this was the shallow end give me the deep end any time.

My nervousness was not of the usual kind. I suddenly felt stripped of all the talent and the intuitive sense that had carried me through previous challenges. I was facing the unknown and I didn't know how to cope. Glyn Shaw, a very tough Neath and Wales forward who had moved to Widnes 12 years earlier, came to the Hillcrest for a drink. 'You leave Wales on top of the world,' he said. 'And it is not until you're about to step on to a league pitch for the first time that you realize that you are not on top any more, you're at the bottom.'

Stuart Evans, who took over from me as captain of Neath and who'd moved up the previous year, gave me a few tips but warned me to stand up for myself. 'After they tackle you one of their tricks is to jab their forearm across the bridge of your nose. Just look 'em in the eye and say, "I can take that all day, you English bastard."'

I said I'd probably say 'thank you', instead.

Newspapers were full of grim forebodings from coaches and players. Kevin Ashcroft, the Salford coach, said: 'The pressure on Jonathan will be unbearable. My team will definitely play on him and we'll soon find out what he's made of.' Leeds and Great Britain stand-off Garry Schofield gave little for my chances. 'As soon as he touches the ball he can expect 60 stone of forwards piling into him.' My fellow Welshmen were little better. Keith Jarrett, the boy wonder who'd come north in 1969, wrote me off as not tough enough. Even Terry Holmes, whose rugby league career with Bradford lasted 40 games before injury ended his career, warned me to look out for the 'crazy gang'.

The only heartening news I received that week was that I wouldn't be going to my doom alone. In addition to my family, there were more than a hundred coming up from Trimsaran in a fleet of coaches and cars. On arrival they found that they had been made honorary members of the Widnes social club, where by the evening they had taken over the microphone for a sing-song and had arranged an Over-35s match under union rules between Trimsaran and Birchfield RFC in Widnes.

My sister Caroline rang to say that she and Phil, plus Ieuan Evans and his girlfriend, were coming up on Saturday evening immediately after Llanelli's game with Neath. That was a match I had been looking forward to playing in. I would have happily given a lot of money to swop Widnes v. Salford for it. Robert Jones then rang to say that he and Paul Moriarty and their wives would be coming up after Swansea's match at Newport.

It was like the condemned man being visited by his friends before the execution. When they arrived on Saturday evening, they'd played their games and were ready for the traditional piss-up. I sat there sipping a shandy while the fun went on around me. I didn't want to go to bed, because I knew I wouldn't sleep, but the place was packed and it didn't look good for the world-record signing to be whooping it up on the rowdiest table in the place, so I went to bed and lay wide awake listening to the muffled sound of fun.

Bleddyn Bowen and John Devereux arrived on Sunday morning and while the Widnes team were gathering at the Hillcrest for the pre-match chat and a study of the opposition on video, I suggested to Doug Laughton that he took a look in the dining-room. Six current Welsh internationals were having lunch at the same table. It was a rugby league coach's dream. Oddly enough, it wasn't long before two of them, Moriarty and Devereux, were playing for Widnes themselves. Ieuan Evans admitted years later that he was very tempted himself. They must have been encouraged by the food at the Hillcrest – it couldn't have been the ease with which I took to my new game.

There was a scare in the first half when Martin Offiah crashed into a goal-post but he was able to continue and I wasn't required to make an unscheduled early appearance. Martin went on to score four tries and was the quickest thing I'd seen on a rugby pitch. Some of the press said he'd stolen my thunder. My entry into the game could hardly be described as thunder – a quick flash would be more accurate.

The player who impressed me most was Tony Myler who normally played stand-off but was at loose-forward that day. He was rated the best stand-off in the game and experts had already predicted that I would have to make it in some other position. Tony had the lot – speed, handling skills, deadly tackling and a great ability to read the game. Early in the second half, he was tackled awkwardly and he and the Salford man went down with their legs entangled. Tony had broken his left ankle, and as he was being loaded on to the stretcher he said, 'It's a good job you bought Jonathan.'

I was never to take over his position, not permanently anyhow. They sent on a forward as substitute for Tony, and as I sat there watching what was a super team performance I couldn't see myself getting in at any position. It was a good game but Widnes were in the driving seat and certainly no one deserved to be brought off for me. However, Rick Thackray, the right-winger, had reported a sore arm at half-time, and after he had scored a lovely try about 12 minutes into the second half, Doug signalled for him to come off and told me to get ready.

Rick ran off the pitch to great applause, and as I waited for him on the touchline I held out my hand tentatively. He ignored the hand and gripped me in an embrace that almost broke my ribs. 'All the best, JD,' he roared in my ear. The linesman shouted 'Good luck' and I ran to a spot the Widnes boys were pointing to. Andy Currier had moved out to the wing and I took his place at centre. In the dressing-room, the boys had done their best to reassure me, saying that when I came on I should listen to them and not go looking for the action. It was to reach me soon enough. Just keep your eye on the man you are detailed to mark and don't let him go past you with the ball and everything would be all right, they promised.

Nobody could have prepared me for the next 20 minutes. I was bewildered. The grass was the same colour, the ball the same shape and the posts looked familiar, but the rest was total confusion. Every instinctive move my years in union had programmed into me seemed to be wrong. League players change position continually, a lot of the time while running backwards, and the newcomer finds himself invariably becoming the one piece that won't fit into the jigsaw.

I was getting plenty of advice. 'Over here, JD', 'back off', 'go now', 'watch the offside'. I managed to keep some sense of my bearings by watching my opposite number Peter Williams, another former union man whom I knew, and making sure I was always between him and our line. As for the rest, I felt giddy. My friends in the crowd, most of whom had never seen a league game before, were having great difficulty working out what I was up to.

If I hadn't had the only clean shirt on the pitch they said they would have lost me altogether.

As for the ball, the boys were careful not to let anything like that complicate my learning process. After ten minutes I was feeling more like a formation dancer than a rugby player. All of a sudden there was a Salford player heading for my section of the line. I looked either side. 'Is he mine?' I thought. Too late. He'd gone by and there was a heartening crunch as one of my colleagues did the job for me.

The play ebbed away from me again and Offiah took a pass inside our half and was gone for the line like lightning. It was a tremendous try and as we all trooped back into our half a voice from the stand shouted, 'Well played, Jonathan.' I think it was good-natured.

Then I made a tackle. A large forward named Ian Blease was bearing down on me like a double-decker bus. Doug had advised me to wear a light pair of shoulder pads. They felt strange but they cushioned the bone against bone impact of the head-on tackle and I was grateful for them. I went for the Blease knees, so to speak, and down he went, dropping the ball as he hit the ground. This seemed to please everyone. It was just an ordinary tackle but I was so relieved to have done something right. I could have kissed him, but the look on his face was not that of a man happy to be sharing this historic moment with me.

From then on it was fine. I had a couple of good runs, and the crowd made the sort of noise which suggested they were glad I could still run with the ball. When the whistle went at the end I was disappointed. I had survived an ordeal I had been dreading and I didn't want it to end. There were plenty of bumps and bruises to show, but the elation at that moment was unbelievable.

CHAPTER 14

Champion at Widnes

Jonathan Davies was not the only one to question his chances of being successful in rugby league. Large numbers in both codes shook their heads knowingly when they watched his first nervous steps across the gap. Wales was full of Doubting Thomases, Joneses and Evanses, not to mention the odd Davies. In the citadels of league there was even less confidence that Widnes had invested wisely. In a poll taken of all coaches in the First Division, asking if they would have spent a world-record fee on Jonathan, only one, Alex Murphy of St Helens, said he would. The other 12 replied bluntly that they would have found better ways of spending the money.

There had been few recent precedents for union success in league. Terry Holmes had been the last captain of Wales to move north, but he badly injured his shoulder after only 13 minutes of his debut for Bradford Northern and his career never really recovered. Pontypool's David Bishop, a combative scrum-half who seemed ideally suited to league, was also dogged by injury, while Stuart Evans, Gary Pearce and Adrian Hadley were not finding it easy to adapt.

But, although Doug Laughton nursed him very carefully through his first few months, there were signs early on that Jonathan had the ability to make it. He proved first of all that he could ensure that Widnes would not be out of pocket. His fee for joining them was to be paid in instalments, with a down payment of £30,000.

His appearance against Salford put an extra 6,000 on the average attendance. He then played twice for the 'A' team, who normally attracted a crowd of a couple of hundred. Each of those reserve games attracted over 4,000, which meant that Widnes had recouped the £30,000 within 22 days of his arrival.

That figure didn't include the extra business in the club shop. Before he arrived they had 2,000 replica Widnes shirts in stock. A week after he arrived they had sold out.

In both 'A' matches, Jonathan started apprehensively but gradually found the confidence to make bursts that got the crowd on his side. He scored his first points in league against Hull 'A' on 20 January 1989. He had a simple kick bang in front of the posts and was so determined not to miss he gave the ball an almighty whack that not only sent the ball soaring through the posts but over the stand and out of the ground to crash through the kitchen window of Mrs Annie Goodwin. It was fortunate that Mrs Goodwin was the club's laundry lady and realized the importance of the kick. She received a fulsome apology and a double-glazed window.

Having started the game at full-back, where he found it difficult to function, Jonathan moved to stand-off at the interval with immediate success. He was named Man of the Match, which brought him an extra £20 to go with his £40 win bonus.

After another appearance as a late sub for the next first-team game, Jonathan was given his first full debut. He played at stand-off for the home match against struggling Oldham. Although he scored 12 points, including a very good try, and they won well, he came off physically and mentally exhausted by the task of trying to fathom the intricacies of playing stand-off. He was finding it an entirely different role from the one he had mastered in union.

Alan Tait, who had recently converted from being an international centre in union to a brilliant full-back in league, commiserated. 'Stand-off in league is a position it helps to be born into. It takes a long time to get used to it,' he said.

The stand-off in rugby league features much closer to the middle of the action where he is required to organize attack and defence. It is a duty that involves him in far more tackles than his union counterpart. In union, stand-off means what it says – the player stands away from the hub of the action and makes the most of the space he has in order to kick, run or set up his three-quarters. The qualities that serve you well in union won't necessarily get you by at stand-off in league and Jonathan found it very difficult to adapt.

The only time the positions were similar was at scrums but rugby league scrums allow only limited ball movement. It was much easier for Jonathan to play in another position and to work off a good organizer – he rated Bobby Goulding at Widnes the best at this – and make the most of the gaps he was put into.

There was another hard lesson as he sat in the dressing-room after the Oldham match. As well as being shattered, Jonathan saw that his legs were covered in far more cuts and scrapes than he had ever suffered in union. The increased activity involved in tackling and being tackled plays havoc with unprotected and unseasoned flesh.

'Hang on,' said Eddie McDonnell, who numbered first aid among his many duties. 'I'll get you something for those cuts.' As Jonathan sat around contemplating his battered legs, he noticed that his team-mates were not hurrying to leave the dressing-room for the bar as they usually did. The Hulme brothers, David and Paul, were sitting there fully dressed and smiling at him.

Then Eddie came back into the room bearing a large bottle of iodine which he proceeded to pour over Jonathan's legs. The resulting squeals were ample reward for the patience of his colleagues.

For the rest of his time at Widnes, Jonathan dressed quickly to hide his legs, and when Eddie wandered around saying, 'Any cuts, lads?' he shook his head as vigorously as the rest.

When he first arrived at Widnes, he earned himself the nick-name 'JD' because of his habit of shouting 'JD's ball!' whenever a high kick came his way. His new colleagues thereupon screeched 'JD's ball!' in falsetto voices at every high kick.

Soon, however, they took to calling him 'Jiffy', a name that has followed him since his early days at Neath. A forward named Jonathan Griffiths had proceeded him at the Gnoll and his name had been condensed to 'Jiff'. Jonathan inherited it merely because he shared the same Christian name. It was nothing more dramatic than that and the name had no connection with a brand of contraceptives launched at a later date!

He has had a hard time explaining this – especially after an incident that was embarrassing for him and French forward Jean

Condom. Welsh fans unfurled a banner at a Wales–France international which read: 'Our Jiffy is better than your Condom.'

If I develop as a coach when I finish playing – and that is an ambition of mine – I will have benefited greatly from studying the skill and the philosophy of all the coaches I've played under. Since I've been in a lot of teams, it follows that I've had a great deal of varied coaching; some brilliant, some not so.

As an instinctive player, I don't believe in too much coaching. Rigid patterns, restricted opportunity for spontaneous action . . . many teams in various sports have been throttled by slavish obedience to a plan worked out by someone who isn't on the pitch and probably hasn't been on one for a long time. Such an approach creates negative play.

I was fortunate that at an early age I came under the influence of Meirion Davies, who organized a rabble of keen kids without placing any control on our free spirit. When I graduated to first-class rugby, I came under the influence of Brian Thomas, who flogged us without mercy in training and founded a style based on fitness and speed. But he left plenty of room for initiative. As long as we were fit, determined and courageous he didn't see any need to impose thought upon us as well. He knew when to be hard and when to be sympathetic and he has consistently produced excellent young players.

At Llanelli, Gareth Jenkins was more of a hands-on coach, more interested in moves and the release of quick and intelligent ball than the physical side. Playing rugby was more of a laugh with Gareth.

At Widnes, Doug Laughton created the best side of its day by having terrific judgement about players. Whether they were playing in league or union, he could tell very quickly if they had the ingredients his team needed. He had a great record of recruiting players from various places who could blend perfectly with those he already had.

Once he had them together, he then relied on their individual ability. But we weren't coached as a team or given specific instructions about this match or that one. This meant that Widnes were the most skilled and expressive side in league, but there were times when we fell down as a team when under pressure. It is difficult to have it both ways.

At Warrington, the team spirit was everything. We might not have had the best players, but we were a real team and Brian Johnston was good at getting the maximum out of his men. Unfortunately, that approach only takes you so far. Warrington badly needed reinforcing when I was there.

When I came back to union, I caught only the end of Alex Evans's reign at Cardiff. The players thought he was the Messiah, and for many of them he was. He transformed them as players. But, in many ways, Cardiff were like England. They played a stylized and set game that allowed very few variations, and even when they tried they found that the plan was like a strait-jacket. Terry Holmes inherited the team from Alex, and although he tried to make it more expansive towards the end of the season it was too late to put them among the prizes.

Had Widnes been preoccupied with a fixed style of play it would have been very difficult for me to fit in. So even though I found stand-off a difficult position, I could play elsewhere and still enjoy the freedom I'd had in union. It helped that Doug kept me on the fringe of the action at first, but I began to want to get involved. The team was playing very well and didn't show any sign of being desperately in need of me, but I was getting impatient.

I was particularly sad at not being chosen for the Challenge Cup semi-final against St Helens which was played at Central Park, Wigan. I wasn't even on the substitutes bench. I had to watch from the stand and have never been as disappointed by a defeat in my life. If ever a team deserved to get to Wembley that year it was Widnes.

There is no place like Wembley for a rugby league team to demonstrate the full range of its talents, and Widnes had more to offer in terms of excitement than any other at the time – and I include Wigan. Indeed, Wigan's record of winning the Challenge Cup for eight consecutive years between 1988 and 1995 would never have got under way if Widnes had reached Wembley instead of St Helens in 1989.

Such a claim is easy to make at this distance, especially by a player who was at Widnes at the time, but this one may not be as biased as it looks. I was not in the team which so unluckily lost to St Helens in the semi-final, and I might not have been picked for Wembley, so I can be fairly objective. We were a better team than

Wigan at that point and proved it by going on to win the championship from them by a three-point margin and claim the premiership trophy for good measure.

The reason I was out of the side was that Doug was keeping to his plan to introduce me to the game as slowly as possible, giving me plenty of time to adjust. After my first burst of action in the 'A' team, a couple of matches as a substitute and then a full game against Oldham, I was moderately satisfied with my progress but eager for more.

After beating Salford in the Cup, Widnes were drawn away to Castleford in the next round. Castleford were top of the league at the time and Doug deposited me on the bench again. I could only sit and marvel at the way the boys tore Castleford apart. We were 22–0 up in 15 minutes and some said it was the most brilliant burst of rugby they'd seen. I got on for a few minutes near the end, but the game was long since over as a contest. We then had the bad luck to be drawn away to Leeds in the quarter-final, and Doug said he couldn't change a team that had played as well as that. I was disappointed but I could see his point.

Leeds were duly beaten 24–4 and when we came out of the hat with St Helens for the semi-final, Doug felt he had to apply the same reasoning. Once again, I was unhappy about it but I never once questioned his judgement. You may get aggrieved when a selection committee you don't respect ignores you, but when the decision is made by one man whom you trust, and whose livelihood and reputation depend on his decisions, you quickly come to terms with it.

Other people were quick to sense a rift that didn't exist, Alex Murphy in particular. Alex was coach of St Helens and had been having a go at me in the press for signing for Widnes when I had 'promised' to sign for them. He said we had shaken hands on the deal, but I could honestly say I had never discussed personally with Alex any move to St Helens. As I have previously related, I met their chairman Joe Pickavance twice and did promise to reconsider their offer later when I'd realized my union ambitions. I said that with all sincerity, not anticipating that only six months later I would be facing a crisis about my place in the Welsh team. Joe rang me at Christmas and I said I still had no intention of signing for anyone, which was absolutely true.

It was Doug Laughton's powers of persuasion and persistence that caused me to sign for Widnes. If it wasn't for him I would not have gone. When he heard of the signing, Joe rang up and offered more money but I wasn't interested in starting an auction. I was sorry if St Helens were upset – and for Leeds, who were the first to make me an offer – but you can only sign for one club.

If Alex had taken the trouble to visit me in Wales and sell me his club and his game as eloquently as Doug had, I would have signed for St Helens. But he didn't and he certainly couldn't accuse me of going to the highest bidder. Alex had missed out on a few signings, and accusing me of double-crossing him was probably his way of diverting criticism. The argument became so heated that Doug hit back by saying that the next time Alex wanted to buy a union man Widnes would do the business for him.

When I was left out of the team to meet St Helens, it was manna from heaven for Murphy. He'd already been banging on about my being wasted, and after they'd beaten us he became insufferable, claiming that he would never have omitted me. Others were saying that I might have made a difference. Who knows? If I had played and Widnes had lost they would have been queuing up to call me a flop, probably Alex among them.

What happened to Widnes that day had the hand of fate on it. Only ten minutes had gone when Richie Eyres stuck out his foot in what was little more than a reflex action and tripped an opponent. The league had only recently announced a clampdown on tripping and referee John Holdsworth sent him off; not to the sin-bin for ten minutes but for the rest of the match. Despite the strain of being a valuable man short for 70 minutes, Widnes were 14–12 up with just a few minutes remaining when Saints launched a desperate last attack down the left and Les Quirk wriggled over in the corner to win the tie.

We consoled ourselves with the thought that there was still the championship to go for, and a few days after the semi Widnes had a league match against local rivals Warrington. This was invariably the toughest match of the season because of the intense rivalry, and I was chosen to play left centre with Martin Offiah outside me. I hadn't played a full match for over five weeks and critics were pointing out that Laughton was taking a chance on pairing his two former union men on one flank because neither of us had proved his defensive qualities.

Warrington decided to make the most of this weakness and directed most of their pressure down the right. It was a chance I badly wanted. Warrington's right-winger Des Drummond was not only a speed merchant but aggressive with it, and when he broke early on and I caught and tackled him it set the pattern for a great night. Martin scored five tries, three of which I assisted, and I made 12 tackles, which is a good tally for a back, especially a delicate flower from union. We won 32–4 and Warrington's try was scored down the opposite flank. A point had been proved.

Although I had earned a reputation for tackling in union, I had to earn a new one as far as league was concerned. You started from scratch as a league player and any supposed talents recognized in your previous existence counted for nothing. They would be the judge of your attributes and would let you know soon enough what they thought of them.

In fact, there is a difference in the type of tackling required in each code – as I was to be reminded when I returned to union – and it took a while to get used to it. In union, players tend to come at you from different angles. They do their best to avoid you. In league you get more of the head-on charges, especially if you are my size. It is not a question of bravery but of learning how to align yourself.

Doug warned me not to take on the really big men if they came straight at me. They'd like nothing better than to plough right through me. 'Let them pass and grab something as they go by,' he advised. This is a policy that Martin Offiah became adept at and I tried it for a while. My friend Mike Nicholas, who has made more tackles than most, said I often looked like a cowboy trying to wrestle a steer in a rodeo.

Alan Tait, who had taken the same road a year earlier than me, told me how he dealt with his first big tackling test. 'I found myself guarding our line as a 17-stone forward charged towards me. He had a man outside him and all he had to do was pass and a try was certain. But he came trundling on, his eyes fixed on mine, and I realized he was intending to run right through me. I braced myself and just before the impact I went down on my haunches and went back with him. He came crashing down and they didn't get a try.'

I added that to my list of tackling hints and slowly became used to what was needed. Thankfully, I didn't get many complaints –

apart from those who weren't happy at being put down by someone my size.

This is one area where the two codes are going to get closer. The new rules in union regarding the back-row remaining bonded to the scrum, plus the trend for faster movement, is going to lead to a momentum similar to league. This will mean more head-on tackling which will mean an advantage to those with league experience and help to make union a better sport to watch.

They do love their tackling in league and they make no bones about your duty in this respect. I was taken to task after one of the early reserve games I played for Widnes. I was made Man of the Match but that didn't prevent me from being criticized for missing a tackle. I was playing at full-back and was suddenly confronted with the dreaded situation of a forward running at me with another running alongside him. I did exactly what I would have done in union. I moved to meet the man with the ball, keeping my balance and hoping to force him to pass while I still had time to get to the receiver. But he delayed his pass until I was almost on him and sent his colleague away. I dived and tried to tap his heels but just missed. Had he been a union forward, I would have fancied my chances but league forwards are far more adept at running and passing.

John Perrin, a Widnes fan I'd met in the Hillcrest, gave me a bad time in the bar that night. He said I should have tackled the man with the ball. I argued that he would have passed anyway. It didn't matter, he said, he might have been selling you a dummy. If you'd tackled him, no one would complain.

Glyn Shaw, the former Neath and Widnes forward, later explained: 'It is a different game with different attitudes. If there is a man with a ball, you tackle him. It doesn't matter if he gets rid of it before you reach him. That's why it is pointless trying to sell a dummy up here, you're going to be hit regardless. If you put your man on the deck they'll forgive you anything.' The Warrington game helped to put to rest any doubts that I was a quick learner.

I had won my spurs at the right time, because Widnes had entered a period of ten games in 32 days that would determine if the club could retain the championship. We played at Bradford in very muddy conditions and struggled to a 16–16 draw, and on the following Wednesday we faced a visit to Oldham, who were fighting to avoid relegation. I was chosen at stand-off and I remember the day so well because the Lions squad to tour Australia was announced in the morning.

Although I had turned my back on all that, I couldn't fight off the sadness of my vanished ambition. Perhaps I wouldn't have been named captain, but the Lions coach Ian McGeechan has told me since that he was as disappointed as I was that my name wasn't there, as he had been planning his strategy around me.

I am sure the people of Oldham will forgive me, but it was a filthy night and as the coach drove into the town snow and hail beat against the windows – I had never looked out on a less inviting place, and to think that this was what I'd chosen to do . . .

Perhaps it was then that the reality of my new life took me over. All I know is that I ran out on to the snow-covered, windswept pitch determined to forget Australia and stuff a few words down a few throats. For the first time since I went north I felt as if I had some control over the proceedings. I scored two tries, each from about 60 yards, kicked five goals and a drop-goal for a total of 19 points, and we won 35–16. The newspapers made encouraging reading. Then I turned to the *Daily Mirror*, in which Alex Murphy had a column. He was off again, writing: 'When Jonathan Davies showed what we already knew he could do – ripping Oldham to shreds on his own – he did Doug Laughton no favours . . . who knows, Widnes might have been at Wembley instead of us if Doug had taken what would have been no gamble at all on Jonathan's instinctive match-winning skills.'

Oddly enough, our next match was away to St Helens, and I have rarely looked forward to a game so much. The entire team were out for revenge that day and we gained it in style, winning 44–16 and thereby inflicting the heaviest home league defeat that Saints had suffered since the war.

While it was going on, the people on our bench could distinctly hear a voice from the St Helens bench shouting, 'Get that Welsh bastard!'

They did their best to obey. I got clobbered a few times. Paul Loughlin was penalized for a late tackle on me and Shane Cooper had his hands pulled from my throat by the referee, but I managed a try and eight goals for 20 points. Alex had the last word, of course. He wrote in his column of how he'd bumped into me a few days before the match and told me not to forget to turn up. He was sorry he'd reminded me. 'He murdered us on his own,' he said.

When I started my rugby league career that January I was so nervous I thought the only medal I might qualify for was the Victoria Cross. Four months later I had a championship winner's medal and a premiership winner's medal. I had played 12 full games and scored 123 points and was unscathed apart from a few dents and scratches. Even more satisfying was that I felt I had passed the first hurdle of acceptance. Rival fans still shouted, 'Get your nose onside, Davies,' but they no longer doubted the physical commitment I was able to give to the game. That was important to me, as it has been all my life.

A year later, which was 18 months after I had changed codes, I had added two Charity Shield medals, a World Club Championship medal, another premiership, and five Test appearances for Great Britain on the 1990 tour of Papua New Guinea and New Zealand, in which I was top scorer.

The heavy load of doubts I had carried into the game had been dispelled, one by one, but I still had one slight worry: I hadn't found a regular position. In my year I played in each of the seven back positions and didn't stop long enough in any of them to feel at home. That said something about my versatility, I suppose, but it said more about that Widnes team. They didn't have any vacancies. I just filled in when someone was injured or needed a rest.

I admired the team so much. It was like playing for Wales every week, except that Wales sometimes have players who are not quite up to it, and the Widnes side never did.

When Tony Myler, their international stand-off, broke his leg in my debut match you might have thought they would be weakened as a result. David Hulme moved from scrum-half to take his place and won the Rugby League Player of the Year title. His brother Paul, who played hooker for Great Britain, took over at scrum-half and was brilliant. The centres Darren Wright and Andy Currier were among the best in the country. On one wing we had Martin Offiah, and on the other was the very strong and pacey Rick Thackray. At full-back, Alan Tait had no equal.

Most of the forwards could play in the backs and often did. The hooker Phil McKenzie could run and kick better than most threequarters. Mike O'Neil could change from a big and powerful second-row to a flying winger in a flash. Kurt Sorensen, the captain, was the best prop in the world. Joe Grima and Derek Pyke could tackle like tanks and produce the most subtle attacking surges, while Richie Eyres, who became a colleague in the Welsh team, regularly pipped them all to the Man of the Match awards. Barry Dowd could step into almost any position on the field, while among the up-and-coming youngsters was David Myers, who scored a hat-trick on his debut at 17.

I couldn't have learned my trade in a better team or among better men, and I was proud to be a part of it when we won three major trophies in 1989, which went a long way towards compensating for failing to reach Wembley. I had been there as a bewildered onlooker when Wigan beat Widnes in the John Player Special Trophy at Bolton when I first signed. Now came the chance for revenge in the last game of the season when we needed a victory over Wigan at Naughton Park to clinch the championship. Defeat, and Wigan would win it.

Had the Widnes committee agreed, the match could have been switched to Everton's ground at Goodison Park, where a crowd of over 30,000 could have been guaranteed. But they decided to keep faith with the Naughton Park regulars even though their cramped stadium could take no more than 16,000. It was a decision that pleased the players. It is not the grandest ground in the world but it's a great place to play rugby and have it appreciated.

Our fans weren't all that appreciative when we let Wigan through for a try in the first minute. I then proceeded to miss two penalties and a conversion, but we gradually got on top and finished up winning 32–18. At the time, I thought it was the hardest match I'd ever played in. The pace and commitment never let up for a second. I'd had a torn thigh muscle for a few weeks and if I'd been back in union I doubt if I'd have played. But I was just one of half a dozen players on either side who carried an injury into the match. It was the sort of game you'd need a death certificate to be allowed to miss.

We were hoping to meet Wigan in the premiership, an end of season knock-out tournament for the top eight in the division, but they were knocked out by St Helens. We won the event by beating Hull, who had my Llanelli predecessor Gary Pearce at stand-off,

18–10 in the final. As a soccer fan I got an extra thrill in picking up my medal because the premiership final is played at Old Trafford.

Three months later, I was playing at Anfield in the Charity Shield curtain-raiser to the new season. It is played between the championship team and the Challenge Cup holders, so once again we were matched against Wigan. A 17,000 crowd saw us win 27–22, and we followed that by making an excellent start to the season, winning the first five matches in which I scored five tries and 29 goals.

Then it was back to Old Trafford for the eagerly awaited World Club Championship between ourselves and the Australian champions Canberra Raiders. It was not the fairest encounter of all. Canberra had just finished their season while we were just starting ours. The Aussies, however, consider themselves a cut above us and not even a flight across the world dimmed their confidence. They began like a whirlwind, playing rugby so fast and skilful that we couldn't lay a hand on them.

Even our most fervent fans thought we were in for the pasting of a lifetime. We would have agreed with them, so shocked were we by the ferocity of their start. We slowly edged our way into the game, but it took a collective effort of application and will-power you had to be part of to appreciate. They were a tremendous team, but we somehow reduced their rampaging to a manageable level.

In the second half their pace began to wilt and I was involved in a famous incident that became literally a turning-point. We were attacking down the right and I took a pass only a few yards from the line. From nowhere came a Canberra back – I later discovered it was Laurie Daley – who swung his arm at neck height and I cartwheeled through the air like a rag doll. I landed on my backside with a jolting thump, facing back the way I'd come. Although feeling decidedly groggy, I noticed a fracas going on between my incensed team-mates and Daley. Then I realized I was sitting on the goal-line and still had the ball in my hands. I touched it down and was sitting there with a dazed but triumphant grin on my face when the referee quelled the riot and noticed me.

Some reports said that he awarded a penalty try, but I can vouch for the fact that it was a proper try, if hardly a conventional one. I also scored three goals, one from the touchline, and we ran out 30–18 winners. David Watkins described the match as 'quite simply the greatest match I've seen, amateur or professional', and there was general agreement that there was nothing to stop Widnes dominating the British scene for a long time to come.

As it happened, we couldn't dominate our grannies for weeks afterwards. We lost five out of the next seven games. Various theories were put forward for our slump, including arrogance and complacency. But I was certain it was a reaction to the sheer mental and physical exertion of overcoming Canberra. Wigan suffered a similar lapse after they beat Manly in 1987. That sort of match should always be played at the end of the season – which in future it will be, of course, since our seasons now coincide.

We did manage to win the premiership again that season, but 1990 stands out in my career mainly because I was chosen for the Great Britain squad to tour Papua New Guinea and New Zealand. I still hadn't found a regular place for myself in the Widnes team, and perhaps my utility status was what appealed to them. A number of players had pulled out through injury and there were mutterings that a six-week tour was too long for a squad that was a little inexperienced. But I jumped at the chance of spending that time totally immersed in the game, and it turned out that coach Malcolm Reilly and his staff organized and motivated us so well that it was a great success.

I felt twice the player when I came back. Papua was tougher than my experiences with Wales in Tonga and Samoa. And returning to New Zealand two years after the Welsh disaster gave me a chance for some personal revenge. They don't profess to take league as seriously as union, but there is evidence that they are avid watchers of it on television. We won the Test series against New Zealand 2–1. On the tour I played nine out of the 15 games, scoring six tries out of a total of 92 points, and I finally buried my last fears about my unsuitability for league.

CHAPTER 15

Welsh Wizard in Oz

In the summer of 1991 Jonathan accepted a challenge that many thought was dangerous and unnecessary. He had already achieved the impossible. After only his second full season in rugby league he had broken the Widnes points record and had been named First Division Player of the Year, a coveted title voted for by the players themselves. He was the first Welshman to win it, and if the team's rewards didn't match his, they came very close. Narrowly pipped by Wigan for the league championship, Widnes were once more knocked out of the Challenge Cup at the semi-final stage by their bogey team St Helens.

Doug Laughton was doomed never to take his all-star team to Wembley. Later that summer he decided to accept a lucrative offer to coach Leeds, where there was tempting scope to build another great team. It was a bitter irony that when Widnes finally made it to Wembley two years later, the team they beat in the semi-final was Laughton's Leeds!

Laughton's last act in shaping Jonathan's fast maturing league career was to arrange for him to play in Australia that summer. For all Jonathan's accomplishments, this did not look very wise. The Winfield Cup competition was undoubtedly the toughest in the world, and the Australian touring team under their fearsome centre Mal Meninga had pulverized their way around Britain that winter to underline the gap in power and skill that existed between the two countries. Jonathan had just completed an exhausting season in which he played in all 34 matches, scoring a club record 342 points. Surely, the last thing he needed was to play on through the summer and into the next season without a break?

He jumped at the chance. He'd been slightly miffed at not featuring more in the Great Britain team that lost two out of the three Tests against the Kangaroos. He had been overlooked in the first two and got on only as a substitute in the third. Laughton, too, thought a spell in Australia would complete Jonathan's education in league and arranged that he should join Canter-bury-Bankstown, on the outskirts of Sydney. Laughton had himself played for Canterbury and had retained a friendship with the man who had become their chief executive, Peter Moore.

Moore had been interested in acquiring Jonathan the previous summer, but Doug had felt that Jonathan was not yet ready for the rigours of the Winfield Cup. 'He needs another season here and to develop his upper body strength more before he faces your lot,' he told Moore.

The Australian was back the following year and this time Laughton relented. There were better and stronger teams that Jonathan could have joined, but Laughton knew that Moore would look after the player. Canterbury, 'The Bulldogs', were delighted by their capture. Prior to that season, their first team had been pillaged by former coaches. Five players, including three internationals, had gone to Wests, and another two had gone to Penrith.

New coach Chris Anderson, who had played for Widnes in the 1975 Challenge Cup Final along with Laughton and Jim Mills, had done very well in developing younger players, but he told Moore that they needed one class player to be competitive. They decided to go for Jonathan and warned him that he'd have to take over the kicking duties. They were very impressed when he asked them to send him the type of ball used in the Winfield Cup so that he could put in a couple of weeks' practice with it before he came.

By the time Jonathan, already nicknamed the 'Welsh Wizard' by the Australian press, reached his new club, the season was well under way and although Canterbury were playing well for an inexperienced side they were near the bottom of the table. He arrived on a Thursday and found that the Bulldogs were due to play none other than Canberra Raiders on the Sunday.

Anderson had planned to give him some time to acclimatize, but an injury forced him to ask Jonathan to step immediately into the team at full-back. Although a touch bemused by jet-lag (he confessed afterwards that he literally didn't know what day it was), Jonathan was an instant hit with the Canterbury supporters. He treated them to two typically scintillating runs that led to tries, caught every high ball that Canberra tested him with and brought off several important tackles, including one on Mal Meninga that brought the 17-stone Australia and Canberra captain to a halt a few yards from a certain try.

Canterbury were winning 16–12 with two minutes to go when Canberra hit them with a late try and conversion to win 18–16. It was left to Canberra's coach Tim Sheen to pay Jonathan the most meaningful of all the compliments he received. 'I'm glad we played them while he was still jet-lagged. They're going to be a tough team from now on,' said Sheen.

So it proved. Canterbury went on to make the play-offs, and that season proved to be the launch of a very successful period for the club. Peter Moore, known as the 'Bullfrog', is a well-known figure in Australian rugby league circles and even five years later was enthusing about Jonathan's contribution:

'When Jonathan arrived he was under enormous pressure but he settled in very quickly. Fellow players and supporters quickly warmed to his constant good humour, quick wit and a very professional approach to our needs. We didn't have to wait for too long to see why he was called 'the Welsh Wizard'. From his first game, he gave his all for our cause. Our supporters thrilled to his brilliance, his pace, his beautifully balanced running style and sensational side-steps. When in full flight, his pride and self-confidence were so great that, at times, he appeared contemptuous of would-be tacklers. His determination in defence and great goalkicking were mere bonuses.

'Jonathan kept his best to last. In the final round, after a string of victories, we had to beat Cronulla to make the play-offs. At half-time, we were behind 16–0.

'The second half belonged to Jonathan. He scored a neat kick-and-chase special to get us back in the game, kicked goals and finished off with a 70-metre try that will live in the memories of all our supporters. There were clever dummy passes, lightning side-steps, pace, change of pace and, 70 metres later, the side that was plundered was in the play-offs. I know the Cronulla full-back very well and even when I see him nowadays I ask, "Have you found Jonathan Davies yet?"

'In the play-offs, against Wests and all our former players, Jonathan was again the star, but it finished on a sour note.

Jonathan broke through, with us only two points behind, and had a clear run to the line. The final bell rang before he got there, and the referee called a halt to the game. It was a very controversial decision.

'Jonathan Davies was wonderful for Canterbury. He came to a club not expected to do well and he could have taken it easy. But that was not in keeping with the depth of personal pride that only champions possess. Jonathan left us with wonderful memories of "the Welsh Wizard" and, furthermore, he had contributed so much to a springboard that was to return Canterbury-Bankstown to the glory days of the Eighties.

'When I shook hands with Jonathan and his beautiful wife Karen on their departure, I had tears in my eyes.'

One of the great breakthroughs of my rugby league career was to graduate from being a Welsh bastard to being a Pommie bastard. The Australians don't make distinctions between the British. Not that I minded in the least. My experiences with Australians and Australia have been among the most valued of my life. I spent two summers playing there and Karen and I and the kids loved every minute. We were very close to staying there permanently, and it is not impossible that I shall play there again as part of a contract I signed with the Australian Rugby League.

My favourite Australian memory, however, is of a game that took place in Britain. It was the first Test of the Kangaroos' tour of 1994 which was played at Wembley on 22 October, two days before my 32nd birthday. The Aussies had started their tour in the usual rampaging way. In their first match against Cumbria they were 16 points up in less than seven minutes and ran in nine tries to win 52–8. They then hit Leeds with another nine tries to win 48–6 at Headingley. They'd reached 100 points in their first two games.

Then they met Wigan in a match that was billed as the fourth Test and won a 30–20 victory that was more comfortable than it looks. By the time the first Test came along they had bedded down very nicely into a triumphant tour.

I'd made one previous Test appearance against Australia, but only as substitute in the third Test at Leeds in 1990, when we were beaten 14–0. So I was thrilled to be chosen as full-back by the coach Ellery Hanley for the Wembley game. I had played full-back in the three Tests against New Zealand a year earlier and it was a position I enjoyed at international level.

It was clear we were going to be up against it, but two incidents occurred that made our survival look impossible. In the 23rd minute, Darrell Powell went off with a dead leg, which meant a reshuffle with Phil Clarke moving from loose forward to stand-off. Before that the game had been stuck at 0–0 with neither team getting the upper hand, but the Australians began to look menacing, and when their big and quick second-row Bradley Clyde got the ball after a cutting move a score seemed certain. Then our captain Shaun Edwards flung a despairing arm at Bradley and caught him high up on his head. Clyde was poleaxed, and although he returned to the field he collapsed at the interval and was taken to hospital.

I am sure that Shaun's action was mainly reflex because he'd been caught off-balance, but the referee, Graham Annesley, had no option but to send him off. It was a devastating moment for him and us. He was the first league international to be sent off at Wembley and the first British captain to go in 109 Tests against Australia. But we weren't interested in those statistics as much as the fact that we'd lost a leader who was both an inspiration and a superb organizer.

Ellery had the idea of taking off a forward, Andy Farrell, and bringing on Bobby Goulding, a scrum-half who loved a battle and had the ability to do a bit of inspirational organizing himself. But to give Australia an extra man for 55 minutes was inviting big trouble. We all had to grit our teeth and do that extra bit.

Five minutes later I had come into the line as the extra man when Goulding began a set of six tackles by passing to me from the play-the-ball. The last thing rugby league players expect, or like, is someone kicking on first tackle. They prefer to retain the ball carefully for the first two or three tackles in order to set up a position. They believe that possession is too precious to take chances early in the set.

But my instinctive love of the unexpected took over again. I noticed there was a massive space down our right flank because they obviously weren't expecting a kick. Knowing I had Gary Connolly and Jason Robinson outside me, I decided to go for a long kick and chase. To this day I think there was a try on, because their full-back Brett Mullins was towards the centre of the pitch. We'll never know, because as I hared after it Paul Sironen ran in front of me for a deliberate obstruction. The Aussies complained that I'd run into Sironen purposely – as if I'd be daft enough to do that, considering how big he is!!

The referee had no doubt about it and gave us a penalty where the ball had landed. From out on the right, I put the ball through the posts to give us a 2–0 lead, which was a massive psychological boost so soon after losing Shaun.

Five minutes later, I was presented with an almost identical situation. We were just inside our own half and I came up into the line at the start of a new set of six, and once more I took the pass. It was one of those moments when my instinct had me moving before I knew it. Brad Fittler seemed to be hanging back ahead of me to the left, keeping an eye on Denis Betts, while the centre Steve Renouf had come forward a bit and had one eye on me and the other on Connolly, to whom I was shaping to pass the ball even as the ball entered my hands.

There was that same yawning gap, almost a quarter of the pitch behind them. So I just went. Renouf had bought my dummy to Gary and I was in clear ground. I can still remember the thoughts racing through my mind. I had two options. I could run at Mullins, draw him and pass inside or I could run straight and trust that Jason Robinson or Gary would come galloping on the outside.

Then, something else flashed through my mind. I'd been in this situation before. I was one on one with Mullins a year or so earlier in the Pepsi World Sevens tournament in Sydney. Brett was rated the fastest full-back in the world, but he is also very tall and consequently not so nimble on his feet. When I made my break in Sydney he was moving to cut me off when I stood him up; in other words, I feinted to move inside and he stopped and tried to adjust his feet to cover the change of direction and I just continued on my original course and got there before him.

I decided to do exactly the same thing. I stood him up again. The try has been shown a thousand times on television, and I doubt if many have noticed the little feint I give as I'm pelting down the field. It is hardly noticeable but it is enough to stand Brett up, to make him check for a micro-second in case I'm going to cut inside. Those split seconds of doubt in an opponent's mind are gold-dust. I came off my left foot and went for the outside.

As I approached the line he was coming like a train and I did what Martin Offiah, the world's best finisher, always did. I angled my body into the pitch. If you do the natural thing and angle your body away from the tackler, he will find it much easier to smash you over the touchline. If your body is angled against him you can withstand the impact better. Brett got his hands on me, but I knew from two yards out that I was going over that line and I did. If I had gone for that corner without that feint, he'd have nailed me.

Wembley at that moment burst into a roar of delight I can't describe. We were jumping about like lunatics. There was still a long way to go, but from a desperate situation we had manufactured a fascinating game of rugby.

My lungs were still heaving with the effort of keeping up with my legs when I attempted to add the conversion. Nobody seemed to mind that I missed.

I have fond memories of various tries for several reasons, but if I had to remember only one at the expense of all the others, I would choose that one. Not just because I was proud of the speed at which my brain assessed the situation so correctly, but because of the very difficult situation we were in and the fact that the try gave us the will to go on and win a famous victory. There is also the fact that it was against the Aussies. I love them but, more than anything, I love getting one over on them. It doesn't happen very often.

The only problem is that when people see or read about that try, they think that's it. That's what beat the Australians. It took an awful lot more, believe me. In the second half they came at us in wave after wave. I consider that, valuable as my try had been, I made a bigger contribution in the second half when I joined the boys in the tackling stint to end all tackling stints.

Unfortunately, I had to abandon them while there were still 20 minutes to go. I had put in a number of vital tackles, including at least two certain try-savers on Allan Langer, and was enjoying the battle when one of my own men, prop Barrie McDermott, fell on me during a hectic last-ditch stand, and inflicted a shoulder injury that put me out of action for weeks.

I was reluctant to leave but I had no choice. While I was receiving treatment in the dressing-room, I could hear the cheers as the crowd urged on the boys to keep them out. With nine minutes to go Renouf scored a try that Meninga failed to convert and the score hung at 6–4 until, with two minutes left, we had a penalty which Bobby Goulding put over with commendable accuracy under pressure and we won 8–4.

One of the cheers I heard from the treatment bench was that which greeted the news that I had been named Man of the Match. I was delighted at the award but mindful of the fact that there were a few other deserving cases, none more so than hooker Lee Jackson who was brilliant at acting half-back and also put in a massive total of 42 tackles.

Sadly, Australia soon recovered from the defeat, the only one out of 14 matches, and my injury kept me out of the second and third Tests, both of which they won to take the series. I also missed the Welsh game against them at Cardiff, where we were too depleted by injury both before and during the game to have a realistic chance.

I was particularly sorry not to be fit to play in the third Test, which Australia won 23–4 to take the series. I mean no offence to the players who were on the field, but I think I could have swung that game. I was in the commentary box – where it is very easy to score tries – and the game was very even for the first hour. But for 15 minutes either side of the interval the game abounded with possibilities I think I could have taken advantage of. It sounds ridiculous but, just as I get instincts when I am on the pitch, I saw situations there that I knew I could have scored from. It remains a big regret to me that I wasn't playing.

If that appears to reveal an unnatural desire to beat them, I can only say that I learned that attitude when I was playing in Australia. It happens to equate with my own distaste for losing which I inherited from my father. But they don't use the competitive edge in a nasty way; they use it to bring out the fun. They are competitive in training. They want to win all the time, and I think it is the way to be in professional sport. It is the only way to get real enjoyment out of it.

It is something we need to address in Britain, in both codes. There is nothing wrong in wanting to be good – and to win.

I'd always admired Australian rugby league from afar, so when the chance came for me to go out and play for Canterbury-Bankstown I jumped at it. I know I'd had a hard season but I felt I was still learning and Doug Laughton thought the experience was just what I needed at that stage. He was exactly right.

Canterbury were an excellent club, and in Peter Moore they had one of the great characters of the Australian game. We had a beach-side flat in Cronulla and despite it being winter we had great fun. Sydney was less than half an hour's drive away. And the team I was in had excellent players. Terry Lamb, the captain, was a favourite of mine even before I got there. The New Zealander Jarrod McCracken was a super player, as was Bruce McGuire, who later played with me at Warrington.

The Canterbury club was a town in itself. When you walked in, it was like entering the reception hall of a swish hotel. There was a bistro on the right, a shop and video rental. Upstairs, there was a cocktail bar, a Chinese restaurant, an *à la carte* restaurant and a nightclub. There were also hundreds of slot machines. The clubs generate money for the teams, although the Bulldogs also drew average gates of over 10,000 and had an amazing array of sponsors. We still have a lot to learn from them.

And despite their tough image, Australian crowds are much less abusive than ours. They'll boo you but they don't get nasty. Neither will they judge a man on his reputation. It doesn't matter who you are, you get judged on how you played in that particular game.

This applied even to the officials. I did very well in Canterbury and I'm glad to say they were very pleased with my efforts on their behalf. But I remember having an indifferent game one day and Peter Moore, who couldn't have been more supportive, came up to me afterwards and said, quietly, 'You owe us a good game.'

I didn't much like it, but in the next game I was determined to have a blinder. Afterwards Peter just winked at me and said, 'Cheers, Wiz.'

That's the sort of relationship I react to. 'Say what you think' is a good motto. It helps to concentrate the mind on the job. But I found everything the Australians did was aimed at improvement and the building of confidence. My game, especially the physical side, progressed considerably over the four months I was there.

The training was far harder than ours, but it was more enjoyable because they put more variety into it – boxing, swimming, weights . . . and everything under intense personal competition. You put your heart and soul into everything, and that is why there is always that extra edge.

Before I left, there was great speculation about whether I would play out there again, and I was tempted. Canterbury said the door would always be open if I wanted to go back. But towards the end of that year came a warning that too much rugby takes its toll. I developed hernia trouble, the result of too much wear and tear, and had to have an operation.

If I went back it would have to be on a permanent basis and, in the end, we figured we had too many ties at home. Three years later, the prospect flared up again during the Kangaroos tour, especially after I scored that try. My contract at Warrington was up for renewal and I had a series of excellent offers from down under. The Australian Rugby League were introducing new clubs into the Winfield Cup. Perth Reds were one and North Queensland Cowboys were another, and they both made offers well in excess of anything I could have earned in Britain.

Looking back, it would have been better if I had joined Cronulla, who played great football that year. I advised Cronulla to go for Allan Bateman and he ended up with a three-year contract.

But before I spoke seriously to any club, I would have checked with Canterbury. After I scored that try at Wembley I'd had a fax from their chief executive which said simply: 'You are still the wizard.'

My career was at the crossroads and we agonized for days. This was probably my last contract and, again, we plumped for home. But I had an excellent offer from North Queensland to play for part of the summer and help launch them off on the right foot. I rang Peter Moore, told him about the offer and said that I would keep my promise to return to Canterbury if they wanted me. They considered it, but whereas they would be delighted if I went there permanently, a short spell might not help the team long-term. I could go to Queensland with their blessing.

Had I known that there was even a ghost of a chance that the barriers between union and league would be broken down ten months later I would never have gone. Nevertheless we enjoyed our stay in sub-tropical Townsville. We had a bungalow with a swimming pool and the kids loved it.

Again, the club was super and the fans were unbelievable. People would take a round trip of nine hours to get to the games, and we had gates in the 22,000 region. Unfortunately, they hadn't had time to put together a strong squad and we found it very difficult. It isn't easy playing for a struggling side out there. They do give you a hard time, especially if you have a name. I paid for that Wembley try in bruises. I was so battered I played only nine games.

Three months later, just after I joined Cardiff, I felt a familiar pain in my lower abdomen. It was a hernia, just like the one I'd had four years before. It cost me two valuable months in my battle to re-establish myself in union. That's professionalism for you; everything has its price.

CHAPTER 16

Reflections of a Man of Steel

When I left rugby league at the start of November 1995 I did so with my head high and my nose as straight as the day I arrived six years and ten months earlier. I have no idea how my career would have fared had I remained in rugby union, and I haven't wasted much time wondering. But I do know that I could not have spent those years in a better game or in the company of sportsmen with as much pride and dedication.

I became a much better player, mainly because I followed their example, and in some cases their orders, and prepared myself properly. I worked hard on my upper-body size and strength, studied the game carefully and learned to adapt to the disciplines of various positions. I was a specialist outside half when I arrived and became a specialist utility man. It was a regret that I was never settled in a position I could call my own. But I look at what I achieved and I have to be grateful for a good living and a deep sense of fulfilment.

I am proud of the fact that I gave as much as I received. I averaged just under ten points a game for all the teams I played for, at club and international level, in Britain and Australia. I broke the record for scoring the fastest 1,000 points in league history and gained every personal award there was to gain. But I never played on the winning side in the Challenge Cup Final at Wembley, which I regret. Despite being close a few times, I reached there only once. In 1993, I was part of the Widnes team that faced Wigan.

Widnes had hit financial problems the previous year and had been forced to sell Martin Offiah to Wigan. Now Martin was on the other side and, ironically, it was through a foul on him that we lost Richie Eyres early in the second half. I played stand-off in that game and I wasn't satisfied with my contribution. The truth was that I was marked out of the game. One of Wigan's strengths was the efficient way they could earmark an opponent and nullify his influence.

Nevertheless, we gave them two tries through errors, had a valuable man sent off, didn't play near our best and still lost by only 20–14.

I didn't know it, but that was to be my last game for Widnes who, sadly, had been struggling financially for some time. The club had won the championship in successive years, 1988 and 1989, were third in 1990 and runners-up in 1991. We were up there alongside Wigan and, in my belief, capable of matching them step by step. But Wigan had the money and the support to grow from there. Widnes had neither, and the moment we were forced to sell Martin to them to survive brought the cruel realization that we weren't equipped to take Wigan on.

The season that Martin went, we slumped to eighth in the league. There was a problem about meeting the contracts of several players, me among them. After Doug left, Frank Myler took over, but a lot of the spirit had drained out of the club and he had a very difficult task. One of the ways he could help balance the books was to get me off the wage bill. I had talks with several clubs, including Wakefield and Castleford, but although I was impressed with them, I didn't want to leave. One or two players did drift away but, under Phil Larder, we still managed to finish fourth and get to Wembley. I didn't have a bad season. I played 30 times and scored 268 points, but the club by this time owed me £25,000.

I was receiving my weekly wages of £300 when we won and £50 when we lost, but it was made clear to me that the only way I would receive the salary I was owed would be to leave. Even then, I had to wait until the following Christmas before I received the arrears.

As I explained earlier, I really had no option but to join Warrington but I enjoyed my time there – thanks to the players and fans. In my first season I won the First Division Player of the Year award, the Man of Steel, the highest award the game can give, and the Entertainer of the Year award. We shared a three-way tie for the championship but were edged out of the title by Wigan on points difference. I am afraid I lost control in the match that might have cost us the title. We were playing Wigan, and with barely a minute left we were drawing 6–6. We didn't know it at the time, but that point would have won us the championship. It was a point we deserved, however important, because we'd given everything in that match against the supposed giants. Then the referee, Richard Smith, gave

Wigan a penalty right in front of the posts because he ruled that Paul Cullen had gone into a tackled player with his knees.

It had been a tough game and there had hardly been a penalty for a tackle. Paul had barely ruffled the player when he slid in, and the referee was awarding a penalty that was as good as giving them the game. I promptly let him know what I thought of his decision. He penalized me by advancing the penalty by ten yards. Since Frano Botica was taking the kick, it didn't make much difference. The penalty went over and the referee blew the final whistle almost immediately. I'm afraid that after the game I gave Smith another piece of my mind. In a long career I've rarely abused a referee but I made an exception that night.

We reached the Regal Trophy Final the following season when we were well beaten by Wigan 40–10, but I thought we were just that bit short of playing strength to make the impact we deserved. The club had promised that they meant business, that they wouldn't hesitate to buy the players we needed. I told them the departments in which we needed strengthening, but they weren't keen to invest. They would sell good players – Allan Bateman was one – and not bother to replace them. Kevin Ellis and Rowland Phillips were members of the Welsh rugby league team, so I am probably biased, but they were treated badly and I was a little disillusioned. I liked Brian Johnston, the coach, but I think he stayed with the club too long. He didn't last long after I left. Warrington were beaten 80–0 by St Helens and he resigned, which I thought was a brave decision. I remember thinking that they wouldn't have lost 80–0 if I had been playing, and I believe it. An old head is what you need if things have got that desperate.

After Johnston left, Graham Armstrong, the chief executive who'd given Gareth Davies all that grief, was next to go. He just didn't know enough about rugby league to succeed. I believe that a few of those have crept into the game. Had I stayed at Warrington, I believe I would have finished my career there, and that would have brought me at last under the same roof as Alex Murphy who, with John Dorahy, took over the running of the club.

The best thing that happened to me in my last few years in rugby league was the Welsh team. This was re-formed in 1991 and I like to think I helped towards that. By coming north myself I had encouraged a few to follow me. Paul Moriarty, John Devereux, Jonathan

Griffiths, Allan Bateman, Kevin Ellis, Rowland Phillips, Mark Jones and, later on, Scott Quinnell and Scott Gibbs all helped to build up a squad that carry the Welsh colours in rugby league as they were carried in years past by giants like David Watkins, Jim Mills and Mike Nicholas who have become very good friends of mine.

Our big moment came in February 1995, when we played England at Ninian Park, Cardiff, in the first match of the European Championships which had lain dormant since 1981. Wales hadn't beaten England since 1977 but, complete with our new 'Anglos', we entered that game in a spirit that was to electrify the country in a year when the union team was giving them nothing but grief.

England were missing a few regulars but they were still able to put out a powerful team that night. We made a great start when Man of the Match Kevin Ellis scored the first of two tries and we led 8–6 at the interval. A break by Paul Newlove led to a Deryck Fox try early in the second half to be followed by another from Jason Robinson. We were down 16–8 but we stuck to our game plan and kept them out with a solid tackling stint. Ellis's second try put us back in range and I kicked two goals to make the scores level at 16–16. In the final ten minutes I had the pleasure and honour of scoring two drop-goals that gave us an 18–16 victory.

To clinch the championship, we had to travel to Carcassonne to meet France who had only just been beaten 19–16 by England. In a very muddy game, Paul Moriarty was our Man of the Match as we fought back from losing 10–8 at half-time. I made a good break to set up a try for Paul Atcheson and then put up a high kick which was fumbled for Allan Bateman to score. We won 22–10 and collecting the trophy was one of my proudest moments.

When we reassembled in October for the World Cup there couldn't have been a more enthusiastic squad; players would have cheerfully died for a place. We trained hard, we played hard and we enjoyed ourselves in the bar afterwards! The game against Western Samoa proved to be our finest hour, as anyone who saw it would testify, but it was so hard that trying to build ourselves up against England in the semi-final proved too difficult.

It was not tiredness that caused me to kneel in tears on the Old Trafford turf at the end. I had just experienced a level of team spirit and comradeship that was higher than any I'd experienced in my career. I was saddened not only because it had ended in defeat but that it had ended at all.

I didn't realize it was to be the end of a tremendously fulfilling period of my life but, if it had to end, I couldn't wish for better comrades around me. It adds to my pride that I played some part in reviving the Welsh rugby league team and that it formed the basis of the proposed South Wales Super League team. But, at the very least, I hope the old-timers who got such a raw deal out of being Welsh rugby league men received some pleasure from it. I like to think of our achievements as an epitaph for all those who went before us and who were condemned for exercising what even rugby union now recognizes as a basic human right.

There will be many other reminders of their sacrifice and one is the players who have come since. Iestyn Harris is a prime example. As his name suggests, he has strong Welsh connections. His grandfather, Norman, left Wales for rugby league just after the war and Iestyn has always regarded himself as Welsh. I'm particularly proud of his progress because he was a youngster at Warrington when I got there and I was able to give him some help. Had he been brought up in Wales he would have been a natural outside half. He has a devastating side-step.

Like me, he can play in several back positions and he has a very competitive attitude. Even as a 17-year-old, he wanted to race me for a fiver in training. I had to leave Warrington because I wouldn't have been able to beat him for much longer! It was the same when I went off to practise my kicking. He wanted to challenge me in that, too, and often beat me. I find it difficult to concentrate on kicks that aren't the real thing but he was concentrating all the time. He also has the right amount of cheek. At the age of 18 he was on the replacement bench when Wales played France in 1994. We were heading for a defeat when Richard Webster went over for a try to leave me with a conversion from out wide to win the game. It was Iestyn who brought the sand on. While I was making the mound he looked at the posts and said, 'I'm glad I'm not taking that,' before running off. Despite his cheery words, I put it over for us to win 13–12. In the dressing room afterwards, I told him, 'When I finish, I'll be able to watch you taking them.'

Iestyn is more of a league player than I am. I rely on my speed but he is more deceptive. I wait for a gap and then hit it as fast as I can. He is more inclined to crab across the line looking for an opening while using his ability to come off either foot. He has a terrific future but I'm not sure in which code. He is the sort of rugby player who would be equally at home in both. We'll be seeing an increasing amount of that sort.

The finest player of my time was Ellery Hanley – and I would have said that even if he hadn't picked me for Great Britain against Australia! Ellery was very quiet but he had a tremendous presence. People say he couldn't pass properly and wasn't brilliant at tackling or kicking. I think it is wrong to nit-pick about a great player's game like that. Overall he was the best player I played with or against. He was so mentally tough and his work rate was phenomenal. I thought Mal Meninga was great, so were Terry Lamb at Canterbury and Tony Myler at Widnes, but for what he achieved and the aura he gave out Ellery was the greatest for me.

In union I'd have to say that Philippe Sella was the best I'd shared a pitch with. But you can argue for ever about who are the greatest. It has been my privilege to have been able to cross the codes and play with so many superb rugby players and I am delighted that many players will now have that opportunity without the sneers and insults we had to endure.

Since union went professional we seem to have had nothing but arguments between clubs and unions about television money and the sort of domestic and international competitions the future holds. It will all settle down, I'm sure, and when it does the players will be able to take centre stage again. I can already sense the emergence of men good enough to advance the cause of the Northern Hemisphere once we adapt the style of our game to match modern demands.

I shall be trying to help the Welsh cause in every way I can. We have suffered so much as a rugby nation from the division between the codes but our rehabilitation is already under way. Wales can be a major force again. Whether I can be, is another matter. I finished the 1995–96 season tired and dispirited. But as I conclude this book, in the summer of '96, things are looking up. Karen's improvement continues. I've been keeping in shape and looking forward to playing and coaching for Cardiff in the season ahead.

I certainly don't feel that my unique adventure is over . . . and rugby's adventure is only just beginning.

Rugby League Playing Career

CLUB CAREER

WIDNES	APPS	TRIES	GOALS	(DG)	POINTS
1988–89	12(4)	7	47	1	123
1989–90	29(1)	16	98	–	260
1990–91	32(2)	30	110	2	342
1991–92	24	13	73	1	199
1992–93	29(1)	14	106	–	268
TOTALS	126(8)	80	434	4	1192

WARRINGTON	APPS	TRIES	GOALS	(DG)	POINTS
1993–94	30	21	99	11	293
1994–95	29	18	104	12	292
1995–96	8	4	29	3	77
TOTALS	67	43	232	26	662

1990 LIONS TOUR	APPS	TRIES	GOALS	(DG)	POINTS
non-Test games	6	4	22	–	100

CANTERBURY	APPS	TRIES	GOALS	(DG)	POINTS
1991	14	7	36	–	100

N.Q. COWBOYS	APPS	TRIES	GOALS	(DG)	POINTS
1995	9	1	19	1	43

INTERNATIONAL CAREER

WALES	APPS	TRIES	GOALS	(DG)	POINTS
1991–95	9	3	39	5	95

GREAT BRITAIN	APPS	TRIES	GOALS	(DG)	POINTS
1990–94	11(1)	3	46	2	106

OVERALL CAREER

APPS	TRIES	GOALS	(DG)	POINTS
242(9)	141	828	38	2258

Apps = Appearances: figures in brackets denote appearances as a substitute; DG = Drop Goals: figures are inclusive in the total score.

Index

Numbers in *italics* refer to illustrations
Abbreviations used: JD = Jonathan Davies

INDEX

John, Chris 27
Johnston, Brian 17–18, 207
Jones, Alan 133
Jones, Clive 51
Jones, Derwyn 46, 59
Jones, Gareth 53, 64
Jones, Gwyn 78
Jones, Mark 110, 151, 208
Jones, Robert 34, 57, 62,
    136, 142, 154, 170, 175
Jones, Stephen 159, 169

K
Keane, Moss 128
Keighley 111
Kelly, Ken 14
Ker, Andrew 154
Kidd, Murray 63
Kiernan, Michael 137
Koloto, Emosi 166

L
Laidlaw, Roy 154
Lamb, Terry 201, 210
Langer, Allan 199
Larder, Phil 206
Laughton, Doug 12, 22, 41,
    166–8, 170, 171, 172,
    179, 182, 183–4, 185,
    193–4, 201, 206
Leeds RLC 12, 17, 21, 134,
    135, 184, 193, 196
Leeds RUFC 71
Leicester 148
Leinster 43
Lewis, Alan 93, 94
Lewis, Andrew 66
Lewis, Gordon 85
Llanelli 13, 65–7, 69, 77, 78,
    85, 139
    JD's trial 100–1, 104
    JD with 16, 143–4, 148,
    149
    v. Neath (Schweppes Cup
    Final) 150–2
Llewellyn, Gareth 71
Llewellyn, Glyn 71
London Welsh 82, 148
Lord's Taverners Sevens
    143, 144
Loughlin, Paul 188

M
McCarthy, Matthew 77
McCracken, Jarrod 201
McDermott, Barrie 199
McDonnell, Eddie 167, 181
McGeechan, Ian 170, 188

McGuire, Bruce 201
McHardy, Hugh 128
McKenzie, Phil 189–90
Maloney, Francis 111
Manly 192
Man of Steel award 14, 206
Martin, Chris 126
Martin, Jason 36
May, Phil 152, 161
MBE 38, 4, 72
Meninga, Mal 193, 200, 210
Middlesex Sevens 3
Mills, Jim 167, 170, 208
Mobbs Memorial matches 57
Monie, John 20
Moon, Rupert 67
Moore, Andy 47, 62, 71
Moore, Peter 194–6, 201,
    202
Morgan, Cliff 42, 144
Morgan, Rod 122
Moriarty, Paul 142, 161,
    175, 208
Morris, Dewi 36
Morris, John 10
Morris, Oliver 135
Moseley, Kevin 158
Mullin, Brendan 137
Mullins, Brett 198–9
Murphy, Alex 179, 184,
    185, 188–9, 208
Myers, David 190
Myler, Frank 206
Myler, Tony 175–6, 189,
    210

N
Neath 30, 69, 76, 77, 98,
    102–7, 111–12, 115,
    117, 120, 121, 122, 136,
    150
    JD captain 127–8, 140,
    141, 142
    v. Abertillery 132
    v. Bath 138
    v. Llanelli (Schweppes
    Cup Final) 150–2
Nelson, Harold 171
Newbridge 104
Newcastle (Gosforth) 21
Newlove, Paul 208
Newport 106
New Zealand 1, 77, 132–3,
    142, 149, 157–60, 192
Nicholas, Mike 186, 208
Norling, Clive 87
Norster, Bob 120, 125, 158,
    160

Northampton 62
North Queensland
    Cowboys 4, 202

O
Offiah, Martin 166, 175,
    177, 185, 186, 189, 199,
    205
O'Halloran, Neil 118, 119,
    127
Oldham 180, 184, 187–8
Old Penarthians 49
O'Neil, Hugo 137
O'Neil, Mike 190
Otago 158

P
Papua New Guinea 23, 192
Parker, Jane 52
Pearce, Gary 81, 179, 190
Penarth 49–51
Perego, Mark 78
Perkins, John 125
Perrin, John 187
Perth Reds 202
Peterson, Alan 34
Phillips, Kevin 129
Phillips, Rowland 207, 208
Pickavance, Joe 163, 184,
    185
Pickering, David 152
Pontypool 138
Pontypridd 69, 76, 103
Powell, Darrell 33, 197
Powell, Steve 171
Price, Brian 59
Proctor, Wayne 61
Pugh, Vernon 9, 34
Pyke, Derek 190

Q
Quinnell, Derek 160
Quinnell, Scott 70, 72, 208
Quirk, Les 185

R
Rayer, Mike 27, 28, 50
Rees, Elgan 103, 128, 129
Regal Trophy 13, 207
Reid, Simon 33
Reilly, Malcolm 192
Renouf, Steve 198, 200
Rest of the World 133
Richards, Hywel 'Titch' 124
Richards, Mike 132
Richmond 62, 71
Ring, Mark 9, 31, 43, 49,
    71, 149, 164